Fair Tax:
A Wolf in Sheep's Clothing

NELSON WARWICK

AuthorHouse™
1663 Liberty Drive, Suite 200
Bloomington, IN 47403
www.authorhouse.com
Phone: 1-800-839-8640

©2007 Nelson Warwick. All rights reserved.

No part of this book may be reproduced, stored in a retrieval system, or transmitted by any means without the written permission of the author.

First published by AuthorHouse 5/17/2007

ISBN: 978-1-4343-1462-8 (sc)

Printed in the United States of America
Bloomington, Indiana

This book is printed on acid-free paper.

Table of Contents

Preface		vii
Introduction		ix
1	We're not Stupid	1
2	Fair-tax; Self-embedding	3
3	Fair-tax Not Revenue Neutral	7
4	Finance Your Fair-tax	13
5	Tax Cuts For The Underground and Offshore Economy	17
6	Good-by To American Businesses	19
7	Keeping Your Payroll and Withholding Taxes Pipe Dream	23
8	Prebate, Equal Treatment and Government Dependency for All	27
9	Social Security Everyone Receives Maximum Benefits	31
10	Read My Lips More New Taxes	35
11	18% The True Price Increase on Goods and Services	39
12	Fair-tax Vote Buying Made Easy	45
Review		49
Back of the Book		51

Preface

It is not my intention to throw a wrench into House Bill H. R. 25, *Fair Tax Act of 2005* or the *FairTax Book: Saying Goodbye to the Income Tax and the IRS*, by Neal Boortz and Congressman John Linder. However, I feel compelled to point out another side of the fair-tax, which has not, thus far, been addressed. This is going to be a short book, but well worth the read.

In this, I'll address the Fair-tax, or consumption-tax, and our current embedded tax, Social Security, Medicare and the Prebate. I will also refer to Neal Boortz and Congressman Linder's book as simply the *FairTax Book or The Book*. Furthermore, I'll point out the numerous mistakes, misgivings and spin in this particular book.

I'll discus how the Fair-tax is vote buying, how it will help lobbyist gain more control over our lives, run our businesses out of the country, give tax breaks to the underground economy and drive up the cost of our goods. It will increase the tax burden on lower income earners and decrease this burden for the upper income earners.

I will show the Fair-tax as self embedding, not revenue neutral, and why employers will not pass on the payroll or income tax benefits to their employees. I will also show how, contrary to assertions, the Fair Tax will not alleviate the cost of compliance.

I'm not trying to write an encyclopedia; I just want to get to the point and keep it short and simple. For the sake of fairness, let it be said that any "agencies" I use in my examples are purely figments of my imagination, but they were fun to create. I attempted to keep this examination as clutter free as possible. Ya'll can trust my figures or look them up in the back of the book, where I have placed some charts and tax returns.

We must not refrain from looking at all the possibilities a Fair-tax will have on our everyday lives.

To simply say we will remove an embedded tax of 22% and other sources of revenue for the Federal Government and replace it with a 23% inclusive Federal consumption-tax that it will maintain the funds the US Treasury currently receives, frankly, doesn't add up

This is my opinion, (opinions are like opinions, everybody has one), of the Fair-tax, consumption-tax, and FairTax Book.

Introduction

If It Sounds To Good To Be True,

It Probably Is.

WE'RE NOT STUPID

This will be short I'm not going to give too much time to the cost of compliance, but I will refer to it again and again.

Depending on whom you want to believe it's a safe guess that somewhere in the neighborhood of $300 to $600 billion a year is spent to comply with the IRS tax code. So I'll use the figure of $500 billion. The Book says that's a $500 billion blow to our economy and lost opportunities. Blow to our economy, lost opportunities!!

What! What do you think the people who earned the $500 billion did with it? Bury it in their back yards (after taxes)? The $500 billion is in our economy no matter how it was earned. The Fair-tax will do nothing to change that. Don't say that if the corporations had it they would use it to expand their businesses, the people who earned the $500 billion do that now. They buy houses, cars, food, go on vacations, etc. That money was in the economy prior to the Fair-tax and will continue to be in our economy after. It's not going anywhere. It will cost us to comply with the Fair-tax just like it does with the IRS. Do they think the citizens of this country earning money won't have to report it to anyone? All they have to do is spend it and that's that. Businesses will be collecting Fair-tax monies. They'll have to do something with it. Set up bank accounts to hold the money, hire accountants to distribute the checks to who knows whom, I guess The <u>Internal Fair-tax Service</u> (IFS). They'll have to keep records of customers that were charged the Fair-tax and the ones that didn't pay the Fair-tax. If a customer buys a product from a company to use it in his business to complete his product the Fair-tax can't be levied on him. If it is the Fair-tax will become embedded in his product. The same applies to his business when he sells his products.

Individuals well have to keep records of how much they earn and <u>spend</u> for Social Security considerations. Why on how much we spend? For instance, a persons employer pays him X amount a dollars and he spends X amount of his savings, he pays the Fair-tax on the total amount so the total amount should be applied to his Social Security earnings. Of course records will have to be kept and sent to (I guess) the IFS. By some dead line date I'm sure.

After reading about the blow to economy and lost opportunity, I got so outraged that someone would think I was that stupid, I'd believe it. I realized instantly that The Book is going to be an intentional lack of information, designed to pull the **wool** over the readers' eyes. I don't mean in lies, I'm talking about lack of information, explanation and plenty of spin (blow to our economy, lost opportunities, bull). The cost of compliance will be talked about throughout this book, so I won't go into detail now (trying not to be repetitive). Anytime you mix government and money there will be **Rules** and **Regulations** to **comply** with and that equals **cost**, and lots of it. As we well know one rule leads to another and one regulation leads to another and the next thing you know we have thousands of pages of (simple) Fair-tax laws. Its time to sheer the flock, and I'm your Shepherd.

FAIR-TAX; SELF-EMBEDDING

Let's talk about the embedded tax. As you know from the Fair-tax there is a 22% embedded tax on everything we buy now. The Fair-tax wants to do away with the embedded tax and replace it with a 23% consumption tax, 1% higher. Ever hear the word **KISS?** Stands for Keep-It-Simple-Stupid. So why not add 1% to the existing 22% embedded tax. Then we can do away with the

Capital Gains tax
Corporate tax
Business tax
Estate tax
Self employment tax
Medicare Medicaid tax
Individual income tax (No IRS)
Social Security tax
Etc.

Doesn't sound very feasible when it's put to you this way does it? By the way, who do you report your Social Security wages too? I guess The Internal Fair-tax Service (**IFS**). Oh well, loose one gain one.

Fair-tax the return of the embedded tax. What? What does that mean? I'll tell you. Let's use some cement block.(Some people like to sell bread but that stays embedded in me so I'll use block.) A mason is hired by a builder to put up the block walls of a house. The mason goes to the factory, where they make the block. (That's all this place manufactures it's their end product.) The amount of block he needs comes to $100.00. That's $77.00 plus 23 % consumption- tax. The $23.00 is already added in price for a total of $100.00. (I know these figures are wrong but I'll use them now and explain later). The mason takes the block and builds his walls for a cost of $63.00 including his profit, that's the end of his service. He goes to the builder with his bill of $200.00. Remember he is in the service business and has to add the 23% consumption-tax. Block $100.00 (with $23.00 Fair-tax included) Labor & profit $ 63.00 Fair-tax $ 37.00 Total $200.00

The same applies to the roofers, plumbers, painters, carpet, windows etc. But we'll just stay with the mason. (I'm simplifying the numbers to make a point.) The builder also needs to make profit. His price will be $308.00, to that he needs to add the Fair-tax, 23% $ 92.00. He then sells the house to a couple for $400.00, but there is a 23% embedded Fair-tax in the price the builder paid the mason, plus the 23% embedded Fair-tax the mason paid the block factory.

<u>Welcome back embedded tax!!</u>

I'll bet there is at least one person out there that has their thong in a wad right now.

Be that as it may, let's be fair to the Fair-tax.

The block factory has no way of knowing that the block mason is not going to take the block home to build a dog house for his Papillion, or use it to build a house for a builder.

Unless he has a Fair-tax card , which he applied for with the **IFS** ,(the cost of compliance remember the $500 billion) to insure the block factory would not charge him the Fair-tax. Of course the block factory will have to send a record of the transaction to the **IFS** so they won't be charged for the Fair-tax (starting to whittle away at that $500 billion, hmm), and so will the mason. Lets not forget the builder he will have to report, plus send in the Fair-tax money to the **IFS** (hmm more and more compliance, hello 500 billion). Will it ever end? The mason pays $77.00 for the block plus $63.00 in labor and profit. The bill to the builder will be $140.00. The builder adds his profit of $91.00 for a total of $231.00. He adds the consumption-tax of 23%, $53.00, then sells the house to the couple for the amount of $284.00. They saved $116.00.(by the way the **IFS** lets the builder keep $.13 for sending in the money). As the years go by the couple adds a pool, a screened in patio, a six-foot fence, and an extra room. Of course they pay the Fair-tax on all this and that tax money will not be included in the price of their home when they sell it (Tax has <u>no value</u> and builds <u>no equity</u>).

Let's go back to the block factory again. They manufacture the blocks but not the raw materials to make the block. They have to buy it from the sand company and the cement company, but they're not in the factories back yard. Here comes Coco, the independent truck driver to the rescue.

Coco buys a new truck for $100,000. The dealer must charge Coco the Fair-tax so there is $23,000 of Fair-tax Included in the price. Coco takes the cost of the truck, fuel, maintenance, insurance, repairs (all of these services come with the Fair-tax included) to figure out how much he must charge per mile to the block factory. Does the sand company sell the sand with the Fair-tax included? Who knows anymore! Anyway, Coco delivers the sand to block factory, gives them the bill for his services, Fair-tax included.

Coco goes home and fills out the forms and sends the tax money to the **IFS**. (More Compliance, the $500 billion that would have been better off somewhere else isn't going to get there).

The factory makes the block and all the embedded taxes from Coco, the Sand and Cement Cos. are in it as well. It's the same for every business don't care what it is. There will be an embedded tax in all their charges.

There's a provision in H. R. 25 that no business will be charged the consumption-tax until their final product is produced, and that will be charged to the consumer (impossible). Let's go fishing to see if that holds water.

Don is a fishing guide. He charges $250.00 a trip. This is his final product. He lost all his equipment to a storm. When Don goes to the boat dealer he wants his new boat and motor to be consumption-tax free, the same for the truck dealer, and the tackle dealer and so on. Don spent $77,000. He takes a client out fishing the next day. He charges $250.00 of which he sends $57.50 to the **IFS**. $57.50 is a far cry from the $23,000 the IFS should have received from his $77,000 purchase(God I hate using wrong figures). Do you really think this will happen? Of course not. The truck, boat and motor, and tackle are all end products of other manufacturers. The Consumption-tax will be paid. It has to be. It's all figured into the "Revenue Neutral" portion of the Fair-tax. (By the way that's another fallacy.) Don will pay the consumption-tax. Figure in the $23,000 to his cost. He increases his price to recoup it, and bingo, **embedded** tax! There is no way masons, carpenters, painters, roofers, and electricians to name a few, or anyone else in a service business are going to be allowed to purchase trucks, tools, and supplies all Fair-tax free. The Federal Government would never get the needed revenue, It takes a lot of fishing trips to come up with the $23,000 the IFS should have received from Don's purchases. Four hundred to be exact. If Don didn't pay the fair-tax at the time of purchase the $23,000 is gone forever and can <u>not</u> be recovered. If he did pay it he'll have to increase his prices to recoup it, $57.50 each on 400 trips, the new price will be $307.50 per trip. An 18.7% increase in price (Remember <u>**18.7%**</u> you'll find out why later). Taxes are self-embedding you can't stop them or make them go away.

To avoid the Fair-tax from becoming embedded into a product or service, Everyone in the manufacturing and service business must remain completely Fair-tax free of all their business related purchases and maintenance expenses. i.e.: Raw materials from other manufacturers, tool purchases from other suppliers including big box stores, new vehicle purchases from auto dealers etc (By the way, when does the Fair-tax start collecting?). Unless it's the final product of the manufacture or service provider the Fair-tax will have to be collected by them. <u>**Unless**</u> their product or service is going to be used by someone else to finish their products, then they will not collect the Fair-tax. Think about this. Will the final Fair-tax collected equal all the taxes not collected by all the manufactures and service providers along the way? Would anyone care to put a pencil to that one? Not Me! Tried it, impossible to figure!

I could get long winded about this, by now you get the point so I'll end this chapter here. No need to get repetitive just to make the book bigger.

FAIR-TAX NOT REVENUE NEUTRAL

Economic class warfare is alive and well and sorry to say it will always be here. As long as you have the haves and the have-nots, the have-not's will always want to have what the haves have or try to keep the haves from having it. The way to do this is to take away from the haves and give it to the have-not's so they can have some of what the haves have. I'll explain how this is going to happen to the Fair-tax in that god awful last chapter.

Before we go any further I have got to say it. **<u>Do the math.</u>**

Every American employee and employer will each pay 6.2 % to Social Security on earnings up to $88,000 and an additional 1.45% each will be paid to Medicare on 100 percent of their earnings. I'll also use my prebate table (page 39). I'll get into the prebate later (Chapter 8, it's an eye opener).

Let's do the math. I'm going to do 5 tax returns. Taxpayer #1, a single mother with two children making $18,000 a year, (I personally know this person). Taxpayer # 2, a single person making $48,000 a year. Taxpayer #3, a married couple with two children making $48,000 a year. Taxpayer # 4., a married couple with two children making $480,000 a year, and Taxpayer #5. a married couple with two children making $4,800,000 a year. I'm taking their income for the year 2005 using the 2005 1040, Tax Table and Earned Income Table. I'm also going to use Gross Income only, no extra earned income or any extra tax deductions. I'll have to pretend its April 14 or I'll never do it. It might also be a good idea to go unload and lock up my guns before I try this.

PERCENT PLUS or MINIS CHANGE IN TAXES PAID PAYROLL TAXES INCLUDED

TAX Payer	PMT. IRS	%	PMT. IFS	%	%+OR-
#1	3,348	-11.8	5,017	23.0	+34.8
#2	10,471	21.8	9,833	23.0	+1.2
#3	4,726	9.8	12,436	23.0	+13.2
#4	150,979	31.4	83,847	23.0	-8.4
#5	1,725,619	35.9	552,698	23.0	-12.9
TOTAL	1,888,447	100.0	663,831		-64.8
TOTAL INCOME SPENT			$2,882.232		

Well I did it. (No shots fired.)

The Fair-tax is $1,224,616 short of being "Revenue Neutral". As a matter of fact if we add up the total income of all the taxpayers including the prebate, the figure is $5,418,286. If all of the taxpayers spent all of their income it would produce a Fair-tax revenue of $1,246,205. Still $642,242 short of being "Revenue Neutral" compared to what the IRS collected, and that's with the **prebate included**. The amount of the prebate is $24,289. The total income without it would be $5,393,997 the revenue without the prebate included would be $1,240,619, a $5,586 difference, big deal. By the way if the Fair-tax is not "Revenue Neutral" were will the money come from for the prebates?

Not to add insult to injury, but the revenue from a 23% included tax will only produce an 18.7% return on the dollar. (More on this later, sorry.)

Lets look at taxpayer # 1. Under the IRS she earned $ 18,000 had withheld a total of $1,332 (FICA and Medicare) her refund is $4,680 with EIC,(Earned Income Credit) which gave her a positive number of $3,348 and brought her spendable income to $21,348. (Personal note: Good she sure needs it.)

Let's look at the IFS. She has $18,000 income $3,816 prebate money for a total of $21,816. She spends it all, pays 23% on the goods she buys which leaves her $16,799 if you look at it as a tax return. **Don't.** Under the IFS you pay the tax as you buy, so she will have a buying power of $21,816, $468 more then with the IRS (assuming the price of goods stays about the same with the Fair-tax). I did the IFS returns just to show how much tax is being collected from different incomes by the IFS.

This is were it hits the fan.

As you can see from the chart above the Fair-tax is short $1,224,616 of being "Revenue Neutral". Whoa! Why? I'll tell you. It all depends on how much the taxpayers spend. Taxpayers 1, 2 and 3 pretty much spend all of their money. But taxpayer 4 spends 75% of his income, and 5 spends only 50% of his total income. So let's say just for the hell of it that all the taxpayers spend **100%** of their income. The sum including the prebate money is $5,418,286, 23% of that is $1,246,205. The IRS collected $1,888,447 that leaves the IFS **-$642,242** or **-34%** short of being Revenue Neutral. Wait a minute are, you sure? Yep. How can that be? I'll tell you.

The IRS taxes 100% of all 5 taxpayers income and collected $1,888,447. All 5 taxpayers under the Fair-tax plan spend 100% of there money (including the prebate) $5,418,286 to be Revenue Neutral all the Fair-tax has to be is **34.9%** (34.9% of $5,418,286 = $1,890,981 over $2,534. (The government can buy an extra toilet seat .) Simple, nothing to it right? **23%** is not enough. Well I got news for you **34.9%** is not enough. What! Why? Glad you asked. I'll tell you.

The Fair-tax is <u>not a sales tax</u>, it's a consumption-tax <u>inclusive</u> in the price of an item or a, dare I say it, **embedded** in it. Just like the payroll taxes, out of sight out of mind. When you buy a 23% <u>sale taxed</u> item for a $100 you pay $123 for it. The government gets $23. When you buy a Fair-taxed item with an included 23% tax for a $100 the government only gets $18.70. What! Your telling me, I buy an item from a store for a $100 with a 23% Fair-tax added to the price and the government only gets $18.70. I don't believe it. Would you like me to explain? Before the store puts an item on the shelf they have to add the Fair-tax of 23%. So in order for an item to be $100 it has to have a cost of $81.30. Because 23% of $81.30 is $18.70, add them together and you get $100.00. There you have it, $18.70 of a $100.00 is 18.7%. The Fair-tax is Short **4.3%** in revenue even tough a 23% tax was added to the item.(More on this later.)

How about those tax free businesses and corporations? No way, I'm not going to tackle their taxes. (They haven't produced a gun case strong enough yet). I'll let ya'll figure them out, you should be able to do that (If you have nothing better to do). Did I say tax free business and corporations? NOT! Remember the Fair-tax is **self-embedding.**

Another point, I've talked to people about the Fair-tax and a lot of them are under the impression That the Fair-tax is really 30%. I've heard people call the Neal Boortz Show (Neal Boortz is the host of the Nationally Syndicated Talk Show: The Neal Boortz Show) and claim the Fair-tax is really a 30% tax. Neal will get mad and say its not, and the caller will get mad and say it is. Neal will accuse them of changing the tax or there liars. Then the music starts and that's the end of that. The problem is, Neal is **wrong**. Neal uses the wrong formula for an inclusive tax. He uses $100 and 23% of that is $23 which makes the cost of the item $77. In order to get the price of a $77 cost item to a $100 you have to mark it up 30%. $77 + 30% ($23)= $100 got it. A cost item of $81.30 with a 23% Fair-tax included is $81.30 + 23%($18.699) =

$99.999 or $100.00. $100.00 minus $81.30 = $18.70 and $18.70 of $100.00 = 18.7% with A 23% mark up. That's what all the hoop-la's about. **Neal is Using the wrong formula!** Also remember that the $100 with the 23% included tax will only yield $18.70 in tax revenue, $4.30 short of the $23 claimed per $100.

This will have a huge effect on "Revenue Neutral". I used 23% on the IFS tax returns not 18.7%. The total income spent was $2,882,232 23% of that = $663,831. 18.7% of $2,882,232 = $538,977 another $124,854 short of being Revenue Neutral".

More bad news, look at the summary for the taxpayers and the amount they spend. The total amount spent by the taxpayers is $2,882,232. Under our currant IRS tax the government will collect an additional 22% of that money because of the embedded tax already in place. 22% of $2,882,231 is $63,410. $1,224,616 plus $63,410 = $1,288,026 short of being "Revenue Neutral" ,if all the taxpayers spend 100% of their income the IFS will be short $705,652 of being "Revenue Neutral". That's only for the **Income tax** and **Payroll taxes** not to mention all the other taxes this program is supposed to do away with.

Lets Look at the purchase of a new vehicle, a $50,000 SUV. A $50,000 SUV with the Fair-tax included will yield a Fair-tax of $9,350, subtract the Fair-tax and the vehicle cost $ 40,650. Instead of buying the SUV a customer leases it for 6 months at $400 a month, to that a 23% Fair-tax is added for a total of $492. $492 for 6 months equals $2,952, yielding a $552 Fair-tax. After 6 months the customer buys the SUV as a used vehicle for $38,000(used vehicles Do Not have the Fair-tax included in them). The customer's total cost of the SUV including the amount of the lease is $40,952, $302 over the cost of the SUV brand new, without the Fair-tax. Bottom line, the customer paid $552 in Fair-tax instead of $9,350, shorting the Fair-tax $8,798 about 94% short of revenue expected form the sale of the SUV. Revenue Neutral? Why purchase a new vehicle and pay a $9,350 Fair-tax, when you can buy it under the Lease-Purchase program! (I just invented the first Fair-tax loophole.) This will apply to Trucks, Boats, Aircraft, and all big-ticket items, even a New House!

Someone is going to go absolutely "NUTS" over this, so I'll quit while I'm ahead. I'd rather go hunting with Dick Chaney then be around that cretin someone when he reads this.

We're taxed on 100% of our Adjusted Gross Income (AGI)? The fair-tax revenue comes from the amount we spend. There are lots of taxpayers spending 100% of their income every week or close to it. On the other hand there are taxpayers who don't, most of which are high dollar earners i.e. Sports figures, Hollywood stars, high ranking corporate CEOs, TV personalities, and Radio Talk Show Host to name a few. Anyone one of these personalities could be earning as much as $8 million per year or more. Under the IRS system they are taxed 100% of their AGI. Under the IFS system they'll pay tax on what's spent. Just for the hell of it we'll assume $2 million, leaving $6 million untaxed. The lost revenue has to come from somewhere. It comes from…?

One other little point to ponder over. The IRS receives its revenue on 100% of our Adjusted Gross Income. The government also receives revenue of 22% of the embedded-tax already in place, on the money we spend. Remove the Income Tax revenue, add 1 % to the embedded-tax, and call it Fair-tax. Sound good to you? Not! The government not only lost the 22% embedded tax on the money we now spend, (It actually yields 20% on the dollar, but that's another math lesson) it also lost AGI income tax, plus Payroll taxes, the Alternative Minimum tax, Capital Gains tax, Corporate and Business taxes, Estate taxes, Death tax, just to name a few. Do you think a 23% consumption-tax that only yields 18.7% on the dollar will replace all this lost revenue? The Federal Government receives about 44% of the money it spends from Income tax. The fair-tax will reduce that revenue approximately 50 to 60%, depending on how much money we spend. Someone needs to take a long hard look at the Fair-tax being <u>Revenue Neutral</u>. I may, very well be stupid, but for the life of me, I can't see it.

4 FINANCE YOUR FAIR-TAX

By now we know that **wrong numbers** and **wrong math formulas** are being used in the Fair-tax book. Nevertheless I'm going to use the 23% figure from now on, just for the sake of argument. Right or wrong it doesn't matter, I can still make my point. (Don't want to offend anyone.) I'm going to make my points telling <u>Hypothetical Stories</u> in this chapter and the ones to follow. I could throw figures out there but sometimes that's hard to follow and its definitely boring.

We'll start with the American Dream, buying a house.

Coco the truck driver (you remember him, he hauls sand) and his wife Fran walk into the Royal Mortgage and Loan Company. They sit down with Sean there loan officer.

"Well Coco, I checked your credit and its great, no problem with the loan. We can finance 100% of the house. Now how much is it, $246,000. Ok, let's see. A 30 year fixed at 6% your payment will be $1,199.10"

"What? That's a lot less than we figured at 6%."

"Let me check again. Let's see $200,000 at 6%. Wait the house cost 246,000. Oh I see now, we can only loan on the value of the house. The $46,000 is tax. Tax has no value and it builds no equity. The house is the security on the $200,000. The $46,000 would be unsecured and we just can't take that risk. Even if we could loan on the tax we would have to keep it **<u>exclusive</u>** of the first mortgage. You'll need a second Mortgage on the Consumption-tax, and that, I'm sorry to say, would only be for 15 years at 8.5%."

"Holy Acrobats! We'll be upside down in our house for fifteen years!"

"Not really, your house will build equity in 5 or 10 years depending on the housing market. Your equity and balance on your second mortgage will eventually equal. At that time you can refinance 100% of your house and have no second mortgage or tax liability."

"That means in 5 or 10 years we'll be starting over again, the money we spent on the Mortgages will be gone."

"Yep, you're right. Buying a new house does have its downfalls! Maybe you two should go look for a used house Fair-tax free. We can loan a 100% on the home and you'll won't have a second mortgage."

"Maybe we should. What do you think Fran?"

"We have already looked at those houses, their prices are inflated because of this tax thing. Besides we get a lot less house, not as good of a location and the schools aren't as good. What do you think Sean?"

"Yes, I agree. The prices have shot up on those houses because of the Consumption-tax. Most of the loans we write on them are for people who can't qualify for a second mortgage. Although, you two have great credit. Lets work the numbers.

"Sean, You said your Company doesn't write a second mortgage for the Consumption-tax."

"We don't. But the IFS does."

"The IFS?"

"Yes, the IFS started a new agency just for this (the government loves to grow) its called the:

Federal Underwriters of the **Consumption-tax** to **Keep Mortgages Exclusive**

"Ok, let's do it Sean."

"Ok. $200,000 at 6.0% for 30 years. That's $1,199.10 mo. $46,000 at 8.5% for 15 years. That's $452.98 mo. Total $1,652.08 mo. $246,000 at 6.0% for 30 years $1,474.89 mo. The difference in monthly payments is $177.19 mo."

House and Fair-tax Mortgage Combined

Loan Amount: $ 246000 | Term of the Loan: 30 years | Interest Rate: 6 %

Monthly mortgage payments: $ 1,474.89

House Mortgage Only

Loan Amount: $ 200000 | Term of the Loan: 30 years | Interest Rate: 6 %

Monthly mortgage payments: $ 1,199.10

Fair-tax Loan

Loan Amount: $ 46000 | Term of the Loan: 15 years | Interest Rate: 8.5 %

Monthly loan payments: $ 452.98

Sell in 5 years

Month	Loan Balance	Interest	Principal	Total Payments for 5 years.
Aug 2011	36,340.69	17,972.48	9,659.31	27,178.88

If they sell in 5 years they would have paid payments on the second mortgage Tax Loan of **$27,178.88** and would still owe **$36,340.69** on the Fair-tax. Only paying off **$9,659.31** in 5 years Good Deal.

Sell in 10 years

Month	Loan Balance	Interest	Principal	Total Payments for 10 years.
Aug 2016	21,782.20	30,139.80	24,217.80	54,357.

If they sell in 10 years they would have paid payments on the second mortgage Tax Loan of **$54,357.60** and would still owe **$21,782.20** on the Fair-tax. only paying off **$24,217.80** in 10 years. Real Good Deal.

Fair-tax	Pmt. on Tax Loan	Pay Off Bal.	Total Paid
5 Years $46,000	$27,178.88	$36,340.69	$63,519.57
10 Years $46,000	$54,357.60	$21,782.20	$76,139.80
Paid Off $46,000	$81,536.40	0	$81,536.40

"That's it Coco $177.19 more a month."

"Yea for 15 years. What do think Fran?"

"If I get job we can do it no problem. We'll have to put the children in daycare. With me working no problem. We can also get that new SUV they have on sale for $27,500. Sean do you offer auto loans?"

"Sure do let's see, $27,500 less Consumption-tax of $6,325 we can loan you $21,175."

"What! That's it I can't take all this tax S#@& anymore! Why do they call it **Fair?!** Someone me get a rope!"

This could be a real serious problem, taking out a second mortgage for the purpose of paying a Fair-tax bill. I wouldn't worry about it, no politician with any sense (HA) would let this happen. We hope. The Fair-tax would have to be changed. So it wouldn't apply to buying a house (they'll have to look elsewhere for money to be "<u>Revenue Neutral</u>", and that will take some looking).

Just in case there's a thing called GAP insurance. But I won't get into that now. I think we all have had enough of this.

American Dream or American Nightmare?

Chapter Three touched on the problem of the devastatingly large Fair-tax bills on big-ticket items, and a possible way to circumnavigate a large portion of them, if not eliminating them altogether. What you can do with the $50,000 SUV you can do with just about any big ticket item, including a house.

Tax Cuts For The Underground and Offshore Economy

The Underground and offshore economy taxed finally (bull). The underground illegal activity, Car Thieves, Hookers, Gamblers, Drug Dealers, Smugglers, the Illegal Aliens, the list is endless. When they spend their money no matter how they acquired it, they are paying taxes right **now**. There is a 22% **embedded-tax** in place. Remember? When anyone from the underground buys anything they pay a 22% tax on it now. In fact when the Fair-tax goes into effect all of the underground economy will get a **1.3% tax cut. What!** Not again, is there no end to this. Have you no mercy? Let me explain.

A retailer is delivered a case of beer. His cost is $80.00 to that he adds 10% to cover his cost and make a profit. He sells it for $88.00. The embedded tax is $17.60. With the Fair-tax in place, his cost is $62.40,(no more embedded tax), to that he adds 10% $6.24 = $68.64, to that he adds the Fair-tax of 23% $15.79. 23% of $68.64 =$15.79 (A lot of work this Fair-tax) for a retail sale of **$84.43** (Surprise, Ya'll thought taking away 22% and adding 23% would make the price higher, didn't ya). The IRS price is $88.00 the embedded tax is $17.60 or 20.0%(Why not 22%? The retailer added his 10% after the embedded-tax. The Fair-tax is added after the retailer adds his 10% (got it).

The IFS price is $84.43 the tax is $15.79 or 18.7%(keeps coming up 18.7 no matter what numbers you use, also 4.3% short of 23%, Revenue Neutral keeps coming to mind). So when the Fair-tax begins the Underground economy will get a **tax cut** of **1.3%** (20%-18.7%=1.3%).

	IRS		IFS
Beer	$80.00		$62.40
10% mark up	8.00		6.24
Retail IRS	$88.00	Total Cost	$68.64
		Fair-tax 23%	15.79
		Retail IFS	$84.43
Embedded tax	$17.60	Fair-tax	$15.79
% Collected	20.0%	%Fair-tax	18.7%

Offshore economy, not much to be said here except, another insult to our intelligence. The $11 trillion in offshore financial centers (OFCs) is already being taxed. Where do you think that money is, in a safe in Bermuda smelling of onions? It's where our banks would put it, invested all over the world, including the **United States**. If it was in a safe in Bermuda, when the Fair-tax passed do you think they would send it back to the owners in the U S just like that? These OFC's wrote laws to get it there, and they'll write laws to keep it, or tax the hell out of it before it left. If you believe that money is sitting around rotting, no amount of talking will change your mind. Saying that its wasting away is only useful when you want to spin something.

Another point, Illegal aliens are also paying taxes too. Yes, they send a lot of their money back home, but not all of it they have to live also. When they buy the things they need to survive on, the in place 22% embedded-tax on those items gets collected and sent to our Government not theirs (another spin).

Also if the Fair-tax is passes they will still buy the things they need but won't be able to participate in the Prebate program . Unless of course, our New Congress grants them legal status. If they do, we'll have about 20 million new Prebate checks to write. Prebates, coming to a chapter near you soon. (It's a good one.)

The underground economy other then receiving a tax cut on the purchases they make (-1.3%) under the Fair-tax, they're going to want to get on the Government entitlements band wagon with everyone else. They'll want the maximum benefits from Social Security (more on this in a coming chapter) and the free money give away program known as the Prebate. Some of the Car Thieves, Gamblers, Hookers, Smugglers, Drug Dealers, and Illegal Aliens again the list is endless will collect prebate checks and, the Deserved Income check, if they play their cards right. Deserved Income check (Last chapter)? You'll understand all of this when you finish this book.

6
GOOD-BY TO AMERICAN BUSINESSES

Let's talk about bringing American business back home. It's been said that as soon as the Fair-tax becomes law, overseas corporate offices will be filled with packing boxes. (You bet, waiting to be unpacked!). Businesses will come running back because there will be no more embedded taxes, no IRS, no compliance just to name a few. As we are learning the Fair-tax it self is **self-embedding** . All taxes are. You can't stop it from happening or make them go away. The **embedding** starts from the first purchase of raw materials all the way down or up the line to other materials and services needed to reach the final finished product. Until It's Fair-taxed and sold. They say business will come back because there is no more IRS, (pipe dream). The Fair-tax monies collected will have to be sent somewhere, to some Government agency for disbursement to other agencies i.e. Department Of Prebate Entitlements (DOPE), Social Security, Medicare, etc. Can't send it to the IRS it's gone, so we'll have to create a new agency. The **Internal Fair-tax Service** (**IFS**). And then there's the **compliance**, (I love the smell of compliance in the morning, it smells like..... $500 billion.) There would have to be bank accounts created to hold collected Fair-tax monies and reports and checks to write on money collected. Reports to send on how much your employees and employer earns for Social Security benefits etc. (You'll love the chapter on Social Security, coming soon.) Enough said, you get the picture. (No since beating a dead horse.)

I made the wise crack that, the boxes were waiting to be unpacked, let's see if it's true. We'll create two businesses, one, Big Beer Inc. (BBI), two, Fly Buy Jets (FBJ) they manufacture and sell business jets. Bob from BBI goes to FBJ to buy a jet and meets Jan the salesperson. Bob tells Jan that he wants a jet, the biggest fastest and the best she has.

Jan says, "No problem. I have one here that you'll love."

"Great I'll take it. How much?"

"$24,600,000." "What? Big Radio bought this very same jet for one of their big shots last month and it cost them $20,000,000."

19

"I know, last month was December and now its January."

"What the hell does that have to do with it?"

"In December there wasn't a Fair-tax but as of January first the Fair-tax went into effect, and we still need to paint the jet to finish it. It's not in our inventory as of January First, so we have to include the Fair-tax in the price of the jet."

"How much is the tax?"

"$4,600,000."

"Holy Bean Counters! Almost 5 million dollars tax! My boss will have fit. He'll kill me. He'll make me take my wife golfing. No, he'll make me call my mother-in-law. Oh no, worse than that, he'll make me listen to, The Best Of, radio talk shows for a week!"

"Calm down Bob. Do you need the jet right away?"

"No, (I need a drink), not till next month."

"Great! By then we will have moved our corporate headquarters, sales department, and paint shop to the Cayman Islands. Then you can go over there and buy the jet for $20,000,000."

"Thank you. You had me going there for a while. I know why you're moving your headquarters and sales department to The Cayman Islands to avoid the Fair-tax so you can sell your products cheaper than the competition can in United States. But why the paint shop?"

"That's just a precaution. The last thing we do to the jet is paint it. When it needs to be painted we'll paint it in the Caymans so it will be finished there."

"Why? You know the IRS is gone, so there are no more regulations to deal with."

"Yes, but we don't trust this new IFS. They're going to want their money. Excuse me, our money. So they're going to start writing regulations faster then someone who just slammed this book shut. So we're getting while the getting's good.

Can you imagine this happening? Especially on big ticket items? I know what the argument against this already is. The 22% embedded taxes are gone, and when the Fair-tax of 23% is added, the price of the jet is $20,200,000. Right? **Wrong!** The price of the jet is $19,188,000. No way you take away 22% and add 23% it has to be higher. Sorry it's not, 22% of $20 million is $4,400,000. The jet's new cost $15,600,000 (with the 22% embedded-tax removed) 23% of $15,600,000 is $3,588,000 add that to the cost of the jet it equals $19,188,000. That's better, it doesn't help your case. Yes it does. I'll explain. $19,188,000 is the new cost of the jet with the embedded Fair-taxes it picked up along the way of its construction. Remember the Fair-tax or any other tax is **self-embedding**. There's nothing you can do about it, you can't stop it or make it go away. The jets' cost with 23% embedded into it, is $19,188,000. Now add the Fair-tax to it and the price is $23,601,240, more than enough to buy it in the Caymans. That's a $4,413,240 difference."

OK Fair-tax supporters quit throwing the book at the wall. I'll concede to you, there is **no** embedded Fair-tax on the jet. Take it to the Caymans anyway and sell it for $15,600,000.

If a manufacturer produces big-ticket items, it would behoove him to manufacture or finish that product in another country to avoid putting a 23% tax on it before its sold. Lets be reasonable if it is possible to keep the embedded-tax out of the manufacturing of the jet why in the world would you want to build it in the United States and have to add a 23% tax on it before it's sold?

A $20 million jet without embedded-tax would cost $15.6 million. $4.4million difference is a lot of incentive to finish it elsewhere. Be that as it may, there is no way the jet will be built without the Fair-tax embedded in it. The cost of the jet with embedded taxes will be $19,188,000. To that you add the Fair-tax of 23% and the jet will have to sell for $23,601,240. A difference of $4,413,240 which yields a tax revenue of 18.7% (need to throw that in every now and then). I just got a little repetitive. Sorry. I'll try to watch it. Are the boxes being packed or unpacked? You tell me.

However to every cloud there is a silver lining. The Fair-tax will solve our illegal immigration problem. There will be so many Auto Dealers, Boat Dealers, and Aircraft Dealer's etc. lining the other side of or borders. The illegal emigrants won't be able to sneak past their guard dogs at night, nor will they need to.

KEEPING YOUR PAYROLL AND WITHHOLDING TAXES PIPE DREAM

If. One of the most powerful words in the world. This chapter is going to address income tax withholding and payroll taxes i.e. Social Security and Medicare. As usual The Book is full of mathematical errors. I'd point them out, but I'm tired of teaching math, ya'll figure them out (Glad I didn't go to Harvard).

If the employer leaves the payroll taxes in the employee's check (pipe dream, it won't happen) maybe for the time being, current employees will receive what they contribute (6.2% S. S. and 1.4% Medicare = 7.6%) The 15% paid in income tax withholding (we'll use 15% that's about the tax bracket for $30,000) the employer does not match, he will retain that money, and after all it's his. For this example I'll use a $30.000 yearly income. Take-home pay for this employee is $23,220. $30,000 -15%($4,500) income tax = $25,550. $30,000 -7.6% ($2,280) payroll tax = $23,220. Currently that's the employees take home pay. The employer not only paid the employee $30,000 he has to match the payroll taxes 7.6%, $2,280 so the employee cost him $32,280 to employ (We're just doing taxes, no insurance or other benefits). The employee will receive the 15% income tax no longer withheld. $23,320 + $4,500 = $27,720 a 15.8% increase of the former take home of $23,320. If the employee also received 7.6% payroll taxes his take home pay would be $30,000 an increase of 22.2% of the former take-home pay.

After the passage of the Fair-tax, it's been implied that, sense employers have an amount of money budgeted for each employee, they will pay it to the employee, thus leaving their payroll the same.(It will never happen.) If you were an employer what would you do? Let's find out. We'll use the same $30,000. Remember we're doing this as the employer. The employee's take-home pay is $27,720. The employee is responsible for paying his income tax. He could claim enough dependents on his W-4 to pay virtually no withholding, so as far as an employer is concerned withheld tax is part of take-home pay. He <u>must,</u> however take out payroll taxes. The employers budget for him is $32,280 a difference of $4,560. The employee just experienced a 15.8% increase in pay from the Fair-tax. To the employer it's 0.0% because income tax is considered take home. However the employee is long time and valued part of the business, so the employer pays him the payroll tax that came out of his check. Now he's taking home pay is $30,000. The employer saves $2,280. After all we don't want to cut his <u>salary</u>, he may quit.

Along comes the bean counter, we'll call him Joe, and the employer, Ron. The employee's name is Freddie. Joe approaches Ron and suggests that they promote Freddie to Forman.

"Gee Joe, that's a $42,000 a year job!"

"Yep, and it will save you $10,872 a year."

"What? (Here we go again folks!) How?"

"Ron, The budget for a $42.000 a year job is $45,192. The 7.6% in payroll tax we have to match and send to the IRS. The take home for that job is $38,880, $6,312 less than budgeted. So we'll pay Freddie $38,880. That will give him a $8,880 raise, over his $30,000 a year salary."

"Joe, that only saves $6,312." "I know. When we promote someone into Freddie's job we'll pay him Freddie's take home of $27,720 saving $4,560 + $6,312 = $10,872 in savings for the company."

"Joe, after all this promoting is over won't we have to hire someone to replace the last man promoted, and take on a new salary?"

"No. Freddie is already above the people we're promoting, so he will be doing the same thing he's doing now. We're just changing his job title and paying him a little more, It's the same for the others. When we get to the labor jobs we'll leave them alone and let them have the extra 7.6%. It's not that much, and they need it.

I did a rough figure on the whole company and just by changing job titles we'll save roughly $497,612 this year."

"Sounds good to me Joe, do it, and give yourself a 10% bonus on what you saved the company."

What would you do?

If, (that word again), the Fair-tax is passed, I'd only count on keeping the income tax withholding, after all it's yours anyway. Maybe! One other point, in the case of Freddie (Are you ready for this), the employer could keep the Income tax withholding money also. Giving Freddie a pay of $35,700 instead of $38,800, saving the employer an additional $3,100. Freddie will still receive a raise of $5,700, with the employer saving a total of $13,972. This could be accomplished with each and every employee in the company. Saving the employer 15.2% on payroll taxes and 15% or more on withholding (depending on the tax bracket of the salary for cretin job positions).

I'll ask you again. If you were an employer what would you do?

There is no way on God's green earth that any employer will let that kind of money remain with the employee. Please don't think that I'm suggesting that all employers are greedy or stingy, I'm not. Let's take a quick look at this logically.

Employee			Employer	
Salary	30,000			30,000
Social Security 6.2%	-1,860	Match		+1,860
Medicare 1.4	-420	Match		+420
IncomeTax 15.0%	-4,500	Match		0
Total Take Home	23,220	Total Payroll		32,280
Difference				9,060
Add To Take Home	1,200			-1,200
Total	24,420	Difference		7,860

All an employer needs to do is to change the job title of a 30,000 employee, add $1200 to his take home pay ($25 per week **if he wants to**) and he will save $7,860 on that one employee. A Company with about 12 employees will save almost $100,000 a year (Or more, depending on how much each employee earns) and still give every employee a raise. There is absolutely **no reason** for an employer to include more money in an employees check then he is **required** too!

Last time I'll ask. If you were an employer what would you do?

In Chapter 3, I allowed all five tax payers to keep 100% of their salary for the purpose of figuring the IFS revenue (Can't say I wasn't being more than fair to the Fair-tax).

Prebate, Equal Treatment and Government Dependency for All

In The Book a single mother with two children spends $45 a week on groceries (What do they eat? Rice and water). With the Fair-tax they will cost $45.58. Wrong. (I'm only pointing these mistakes out for a point later. By now you know The Book is full of them.) The cost without the 22% embedded tax is right $35.10, add 23% and it = $43.17 (Remember everything is cheaper with 23% added to it.), a difference of $8.07 which = (bet it's 18.7%) 18.69% (should've bet).

The Prebate Table is **wrong**. The math is right (Amazing!), 23% of $9,800 = 2,254. The actual taxes paid by the consumers equals 18.7% therefor 18.7% of $9,800 = $1,833. A difference of $421 or 2.3% too much. With a family of four the prebate will be reduced from $506 to $411 a month.

The charts in the back of the book are the, Federal Poverty Level (FPL) Guidelines for 2006. The one we're interested in is the first one, it's the one used to figure your prebate. The other one shows the percentage a family is above the FPL. The Fair-tax doesn't have a marriage penalty, therefor a married couple will get credit for $9800 each giving them a poverty level of $19,600 in family unit 2. Therefor I'll have to add $3400 for each child to that figure to come up with a Prebate Table.

Family unit	Poverty Level		Perbate @ 23%		Prebate @ 18.7%	
	Annual	Monthly	Annual	Monthly	Annual	Monthly
1	$9,800	$817	$2,254	$188	$1,833	$153
2	19,600	1,633	4,508	376	3,665	305
3	23,000	1,917	5,290	441	4,301	358
4	26,400	2,200	6,072	506	4,937	411
5	29,800	2,483	6,854	571	5,573	464
6	33,200	2,767	7,636	636	6,209	517
7	36,600	3,050	8,418	701	6,845	570
8	40,000	3,333	9,200	766	7,481	623
9	43,400	3,616	9,982	832	8,117	676
10	46,800	3,899	10,764	897	8,753	729
11	50,200	4,182	11,546	962	9,389	782
12	53,600	4,465	12,328	1,027	10,025	835
Add for additional child	3,400	283	782	65	636	53

Unlike the present income tax system, The Fair-tax treats each and ever person in this country the same. That's the claim anyway. I'll bet the homeless can't wait for the Fair-tax to pass.

"What's that Babe" (a friend of mine in the other room, I can hear her but you can't, sometimes I wish I couldn't either. Don't print that!) ? "What do you mean the homeless won't get a prebate check? No job! What does that have to do with it? Do you have to have a job to be a consumer? When they buy their necessities of life, they're paying the consumption-tax, so they should get a prebate check too. Doesn't matter, they have jobs. What's that Babe? What jobs? Why you see them working every day at the intersections with their signs. "Homeless, Please Help, God Bless". What do you mean that's not a good job, Babe? Why it must be, did you ever see an Illegal Alien doing it? I'll bet they make at least $88,000 a year. (Where have I heard that number before, hmm) Why I can see the signs now, 'Homeless, Please Help, Support the Fair-tax, God Bless'. What's that Babe, How will they get their checks? They can have them sent to their local place of handouts. The Godless Church of the Bleeding Hearts. If they don't get them, those do gooders will drop their serving spoons (Faster then this book burned in someone's fireplace), and head strait to the nearest office of the ACLU. When that happens, grab your wallet and look out."

"By the way Babe, the $200 you send to your son at collage to help him support himself, you'll only have to send him $12, because his prebate check will be $188." (If they don't correct the table). "What? He won't get a check! Why not? Because you claim him! Claim him to whom? There's no IRS. He's over 18, every collage student in the country will get a check. They're all consuming too ya know." (Revenue Neutral? Hmm).

"What's that Babe? Am' I sure he'll get that much, give me a minute to check.

Let's see, hmm, $200 a mo. times 12 (year round student) = $2400 a year, he earns $6,000 that's $8,400, poverty level $9800 - $8,400 = $1,400 he's not spending. Hmm. Will he get credit for that amount? What's that Babe? Yep. Got to look something up in the Department Of Prebate Entitlements. (DOPE)

Let's see prebate, prebate, rrrr, here it is, read this real quickly. Ha! Doesn't say a thing about how much you have to spend. Hmm, that's not very revenue neutral. Ah, doesn't matter, if it saves us from sending him money. Great! The answer's yes Babe, he'll get a $188 a month same as the homeless and jobless will" (More of course if they're married and have children).

Each and every person in this country the same.

If I offended anyone, **Get Over It!**

I'll get serious for a moment. Everyone over the age of 18 will and should get a Prebate check. No matter if they have a job or not. We're being taxed on items we buy no matter where we get our money. The money could come from a parent, brother or sister, a trust fund, or odd jobs etc. This income doesn't have to be reported because there's no IRS. All we have to do is spend it. Any amount we want, ten bucks or ten million, we'll all get our prebate checks. Brings up <u>Revenue Neutral,</u> Millions of extra Prebate checks, imagine $188 to every person in this country over the age of 18. In 2005 we had a little more then 296 million people in the United States, 75.2% are over 18 years of age. That's 223 million Prebate checks. 223,000,000 X $188 = $41,924,000,000 (Forty one <u>Billion</u> Nine Hundred Twenty Four <u>Million</u> Dollars. **<u>A month</u>**)! $41,924,000,000 X 12 months = $503,088,000,000 (Five Hundred Three <u>Billion</u> Eighty Eight <u>Million</u> Dollars **<u>A Year!,</u>** at the minimum of $188 a month.) The other 73 million people are children. Most children have parents, or a guardian collecting an additional $65 in Prebate money for each child. 73 Million X $65 = $4,745,000,000 (Four <u>Billion</u> Seven Hundred Forty Five <u>Million</u> Dollars **<u>A Month!</u>**) $4,745,000,000 X 12 months = $56,940,000,000 (Fifty Six <u>Billion</u> Nine Hundred Forty <u>Million</u> Dollars **<u>A Year</u>**)! Total per Month Adults and Children $46,669,000,000 (Forty Six <u>Billion</u> Six Hundred Sixty Nine <u>Million</u> **<u>A Month</u>**)! Total for a Year $560,028,000,000 (Five Hundred Sixty <u>Billion</u> Twenty Eight <u>Million</u> Dollars **<u>A Year</u>**)! That's more than half a **<u>Trillion</u>** Dollars a year. By the time the Fair-tax is passed there will be over 300 Million of us.

U.S. Population, 2005	296,410,404	(296,000,000)
Adults	222,940,420	75.2% (223,000,000)
Children	73,469,984	24.8% (73,000,000)
Prebate Per Month		**Prebate Per Year**
Adult $41,924,000,000		$503,008,000,000
Child $4,745,000,000		$56,940,000,000
Total $46,669,000,000		$560,028,000,000

Grand Total   **$560,028,000,000.00**

Let's put these figures in perspective. If you spent a dollar every second 24-7, it would take about 12 days to spend one Million dollars, 32 years to spend one Billion dollars and 31,709 years to spend a one Trillion dollars, or 17,758 years to spend ($560,028,000,000) one year of prebate money.

560 Billion Dollars promised to each and every American every year. Our National Deficit as of March 2007 is about 270 Billion Dollars, less then half of the Prebate budget. Passing the Fair-tax Will increase our National Deficit **307%** to **830 Billion Dollars!** Will someone please tell us where this money is going to come from, when every American is spending 100% of their income just to, "almost" keep up with lost Income Tax, and Payroll Tax revenue!

Sending a $188 to people who earn 6, to 10 figure incomes is absolutely pointless. (Might as well put perfume on a pig.) It wouldn't cover their tip in a fine restaurant. There's one reason and one reason only why the prebate is included in the Fair-tax. It's to **Buy** support for the Fair-tax from the poor and lower income citizens. If you're one of these people don't fall for it. The Fair-tax is a:

Wolf in Sheep's Clothing.

The prebate money will be consumed by Price Increases and New Taxes and then some (Chapters 10,11).

One last thought on this subject. **Stupid,** but **Shrewd**.

SOCIAL SECURITY EVERYONE RECEIVES MAXIMUM BENEFITS

Let's discuss Social Security, and how the Fair-tax will effect it. For years all I ever heard was, the more you put into Social Security (SS) the less you receive back. Not true. The more a taxpayer deposits into SS the higher his monthly benefit will be. For example We'll have a taxpayer earning is $50,000 a year, and another earning $88,000 a year. The taxpayer earning $50,000 deposits $3,100 per year, the taxpayer earning $88,000, deposits $5,456 per year. Why is this important? To make my next point. The more someone puts into SS the more money received, for retirement or disability benefits. Both taxpayers paid 6.2% of their income. Therefor the higher one can report his income the better off he'll be. The figures below are calculated from the Social Security Quick Calculator, updated December 29, 2005.

SOCIAL SECURITY RETIREMENT
$50,000 VS $88,000

AGE	RETIRE 67		$50,000	$88,000	$ INCREASE
1. 56	2017	RET. Benft.	1591	2184	593 +
		DIS. Benft.	1299	1864	565 +
2. 41	2032	RET. Benft.	1663	2196	533 +
		DIS. Benft	1426	1976	550 +
3. 25	2048	RET. Benft.	1688	2245	557 +
		DIS.Benft.	1562	2096	534 +
		AVG. RET.+ 561			
		AVG. DIS. + 550			

Three examples are enough, the numbers stay the same, I could raise or lower the salary's but the $88,000 is the highest yield. (Hmm that's were I heard that number before.)

Employers are required send a report on the earnings of their employees and themselves, to the government for Social Security considerations. "What's that Babe? To who? Who knows! I guess the IFS! What? Oh! You read in the paper that the IFS opened an agency to process the reports. What's their name Babe?

The Social Security Headquarters of Income Tabulation.

Got it! Thanks Babe. Yep, just what we need another agency we don't have to comply to. (I know we'll have to, I'm just going by what I read).

Let see my employer sent my salary report in. In the amount of $59,500 I also made a few bucks here, a little more there, some gambling, that comes to. Oh No! That can't be, I'll do some adjusting. I made a lot there, and a killing gambling. Ah that's it, made it, $88,001.

What's that Babe? I'm doing what with the figures? Of course I'm, so what! Who cares? By the way, you have to make $26,450 at your next yard sales, to get to $88,001. What Babe? Report it! To Whom? There's no more IRS and the IFS only cares about how much we spend. Hell, they don't even know how much that is! All I have to do is send a few reports to the **Social Security Headquarters** of **Income Tabulation** and that's that.

The previous may be a little absurd, but it's the best way to explain it. Are the homeless going to be covered by Social Security (no joke), they're spending money, paying the consumption-tax, they should get credit for it, at least the minimum amount. Plus any money they earn from private sources, or any other way. All amounts of incomes are potentiality Fair-taxable (did I just coin a word). Do we have to keep records of all the money we spend each year? Just to insure we get the proper credit towards our Social Security or is the **Social Security Headquarters** of **Income Tabulation** just going to go by an employers W-2. Hold it! There's no IRS, so no W-2. I guess it will be replaced with a Fair-tax form for businesses and private use. Which will be known as The Fair-tax Uniform form, or the **FU-2**.

Are there provisions for reporting extra income from private sources especially cash, for the taxpayers? If a taxpayer is just below the $88,000 will the interest on investments figure in to his total income? If a taxpayer saves $25,000 from the previous year and his employer pays him $50,000 this year, is his income $75,000? It should be, he has the potential to spending $75,000 that year, thus paying the consumption-tax on it. What if he only spends $15,000 of it, is his income $65,000? Carrying $10,000 to the following year. Will we be required to report all our __income__ and __spending__ up to the amount of $88,000, or will they want to know __everything__. By the way what's the deadline for reporting all this crap to **S.S.H.I.T**! . __April 15th?__

I know no matter what tax system we have there's going to be fraud, there's nothing anyone can do about it. But if we won't have to report all of our earnings, it will be just as easy to report more than we earn. Then we'll probably have 223 million people eligible for maximum Social Security benefits. I can see the form now.

Paid by employer	$50,000	
Won Gambling	$50,000	Spent it.
Total Earnings	$100,000.	

When the Fair-tax goes into effect, the Government sure will be surprised to find out how much everyone does earn.

Get my point?

READ MY LIPS
MORE NEW TAXES

If we're spending 100% of our money just to keep up with lost Income Tax, and Payroll Tax revenue, where is the money going to come from to fund all the eliminated taxes Capital Gains, Corporate Taxes, Estate Taxes, Self Employment Taxes, AMT Tax etc.? You guessed it, **New Taxes!** Let's list and talk about a few of them.

Internet: All purchases on the Internet no matter what state or country the purchase is made from, a 23% Fair-tax will be added to it. You can bet if the Feds tax us it won't be long before we are paying sales tax to non-resident states. Don't forget the fees we pay to our ISP will also have a 23% Fair-tax on them. You can include a 23% Fair-tax on all catalog purchases too.

Phone: A 23% Fair-tax will be included in your phone bill, also if your payment to your Internet Service Provider is included in your phone bill, the 23% you pay your ISP will be embedded in that bill.

Cable: The same holds true for cable, as the Phone. No sense repeating myself.

Doctors: Lets assume your Doctor charges $200 for an office visit (To make this point I'll go along with the Fair-tax, there are no embedded taxes and the price remains the same, (the figures don't matter the math is the same for any price) you pay $30 co-pay and the insurance picks up the balance. Now the Fair-tax is in effect, without embedded taxes the Doctors cost is $156, to that he has to add the Fair-tax 23%, the price is now $192. This is my point. Do you think the insurance co. is going to pay **your tax** for his service? I don't think so. Your cost to go to the Doctor will now be $30 co-pay and $36 Fair-tax for a total of $66. Insurance Cos. are not going to start picking up the federal tax bills for all of their clients (especially when its in their favor).

Do you want to do the taxes for a weeks stay in a hospital? You'll have to, I'm not that brave!

Prescription drugs: Just about the same for a Doctor, you'll have your co-pay plus the Fair-tax. You can figure about $18.70 payment added per $100 of your prescriptions. The Insurance cos. probably won't pay that tax either. Oh, while I'm thinking about it, we'll all have to pay the Fair-tax on the insurance our employers provide for us. Wait till you see the amount of that coming out of your <u>check</u>, You'll appreciate how much he actually pays for it.

Federal government: What? Do you believe this? The Feds pay the fair-tax too! Its' like taking money out of one pocket and putting it in the other. I think this is just a ploy to bump up the amount of revenue collected to convince people and also justify the Fair-tax as being **Revenue Neutral.** The argument against this would be that the federal government is no longer paying the embedded tax on their purchases so they should pay also. Even if this was true, were does the money come from to pay the tax, from the Fair-tax revenue already collected (Duh).

State Governments: Now this is not funny, the states will have to pay the 23% Fair-tax on their purchases. The states don't retain collected Fair-tax, so that money will be sent to the federal government. This will increase the cost of operation to the states. And where do the states get the money to operate? From us in the form of taxes, you guessed it again, tax increases.

Local Governments: This is where it gets <u>expensive</u>. Most local and municipal governments provide electricity, gas, water, sewer and garbage collection. When the commissions of these various organizations want an increase of let's say 4 or 5 % all hell breaks loose. There are commission meetings, town meetings and sometimes even a public vote to get it. Now the Fair-tax wants to hit **all** of these services with a 23% increase **all** at once. Can you take this hard a hit? **Not Me.** Just to list a few of the other new taxes on services.

Hospitals

Heating oil:

Beauty shops:

Barbers:

Auto Repair Shops:

Lawyers:

Auto Insurance:

Home Insurance:

All Insurance:

Plumbers:

Electricians:

AC Repairs:

I could go on and on. The list may well be endless. Do you think your prebate check will cover all of these new taxes plus many more, and still relieve you from paying tax on the necessities of life? I don't think so. Most of the new taxes listed are necessities of life. Including the State and municipal government services Electricity, Gas, water, sewer and Garbage collection (A three day hospital stay will eat up a prebate check).

Who will these new taxes impact the most? The poor and lower income families that live from paycheck to paycheck. I don't think the middle income families could take a 23% increase on their municipal services as well. There will be a 23% increase, because the Fair-tax is self-embedding. I will argue this point with anybody, even on National TV if I have too (Of course for a fee, if I was only doing this for the money). By the way, the 22% embedded tax we now pay is it all federal taxes, or are there some State and local taxes in there too that can't be removed? If that's the case the Fair-tax will be a lot more than 23% with the state and local embedded taxes included (I don't know, so let's assume there all Federal taxes).

I saved one new tax for last, because it will effect some people more than others depending on weather or not your state has a sales tax on <u>FOOD.</u> All states have different sales taxes, ranging from 6% to 8.5% (approximately). Too many differences in state taxes. I'll use non-taxed food. My research with real people, a family of four spends approximately $90 to $130 a week on food. I'll use $110. We're talking about food so I'll be serious.

The Fair-tax is self-embedding just like any other tax, so the cost of food will go up along with any other products or services. The increase is 1% over the 22% embedded tax in place now. I won't adjust the numbers for 1%.

Food cost	Per week	Increase	Per month	Increase
	$110		$440	
Fair-tax 23%	$25		$101	
Total	$135	18.7%	$541	18.7%
Increase expense	$ 25	22.9%	$101	22.9

Why the differences in percentages? The Fair-tax yields 18.7% of the sales, the food cost to the customer increased by a markup of 23%. A family of four receives a prebate check in the amount of $506 per month, $101 of it will go to the new tax on food, leaving $405 for all the other "NEW TAXES".

Do you want a 23% increase on your food, utilities and services not being taxed now? Not Me! Keep your prebate check! You'll only come up with a reason to take it back sooner or later anyway. Probably a half Trillion of them.

By the way the Prebate for a family four will be $411 not $506 (Fair-tax yields 18.7% not 23%), leaving that family after food cost with $310 for all the other taxes.

I feel I need to explain the percentages one more time, so no one will think that there is some kind of Hocus Pocus or slight of calculator going on with these figures.

An item arrives at a retailer with cost of $70. He adds 10% $7 to cover his cost and profit. To that he has to add 23% Fair-tax, $17.71, for a shelf price of $94.71. The amount the customer pays, is $94.71 no more no less. The tax is $17.71, divide the tax by $94.71 and the percentage is 18.699 % or 18.7% . The actual percentage the customer paid in taxes.

To find the mark up on a $77 item you have to multiply it by the tax amount, in this case .23. The customer paid 23% more then the cost, But only 18.7% in tax money on the sale price. The retailer will submit 18.7% of every dollar in sales to the Government, or $18.70 on every hundred dollars of sales, it's the only way it can be figured. One more time, just to put the 30% tax bull to rest. We'll use the same cost on the item with the retailers profit figured in $77. .30 times $77 equals $23.10 or $23 added to cost of $77 = $100.00. The customer pays a mark up of 30%. the actual tax percentage is 23% . $23 divided by the sale amount of $100 is 23%. If you want or need **$23** on every **$100** dollars of sales, you must have a Fair-tax of **30%**.

That's it in a nut shell. No mathematical semantics or exclusive or inclusive baloney, pure facts. Math doesn't lie it has only one answer, the correct one.

Fair-tax @	23%	30%	
Cost	77.00	77.00	With retailer 10% Added
Tax	17.71	23.10	% Tax X Cost = Tax
Sale Price	94.71	100.10	Cost Plus Tax
Tax Paid	18.7%	23%	Tax Divided by Sale Price

Go ahead get out your calculator, you know you want too, use any number that comes to mind, big or small size doesn't matter (With math anyway). Then ask yourself, is the math lying too.

18% THE TRUE PRICE INCREASE ON GOODS AND SERVICES

The nice thing about math is, its not prejudice. It will give the same answer to anyone that uses it (provided you know how). It can't be spun to give a false answer, there is only one, the correct one.

I've been saying throughout this book that the Fair-tax is self embedding, and that the price of everything will go up 23%. I lied, I used 23% for the sake of The Book. But the true figure is 18.%. Lets use my buddy and the author of this book, **MATH.** I'm going to build a house, and the figures are going to be real simple (So cretin people can follow it, you know who you are). It's going to take ten businesses or service builders to build it and a builder to sell it. I'm going to be as fair to the Fair-tax as I can no bull no funny stuff (maybe). I'll show the IRS cost and the IFS cost. Here we go folks.

The ten service builders will charge the builder a $1,000 each and the builder will add 10% to cover his cost and also make a profit under the current IRS tax. For the IFS I'll remove the 22% embedded tax and add the 23% Fair-tax, I'll do that now. $1,000 less 22% = $780. $780 plus 23% Fair-tax = $959.40 or $960. $960 OK with ya'll? I'll take out the extra six bucks at the end if you want me too.

	IRS	IFS
Foundation	$1,000	$960
Plumber	1,000	960
Framer	1,000	960
Roofer	1,000	960
Drywall	1,000	960
Electrician	1,000	960
Painter	1,000	960
Floors	1,000	960
Windows	1,000	960
Mason	1,000	960
Sub Total	$10,000	$9,600
Builder + 10%	1,000	960
Total	$11,000	$10,560
Fair-tax 23%	0	$2,438
Grand Total	$11,000	$12,989
Price - % Increase	0	$1,989 +18.%

As you can see the price of the house increased by $1,989 for a total increase over the $11,000 of 18%, even though the Fair-tax prices were cheaper then the IRS prices.

Some people have told me the figures are too simple. OK I'll do it again using more realistic figures. I'll do it the same as above, IRS price and IFS price. I won't do the math for each figure here (too much clutter) but you can check them using the formula from the first example.

	IRS	IFS	
Foundation	$14,250	$13,672	
Plumber	9,370	8,990	
Framer	18,900	18,133	
Roofer	38,000	36,457	
Drywall	20,000	19,188	
Electrician	12,500	11,993	
Painter	20,500	19,668	
Floors	10,000	9594	
Windows	17,800	17,173	
Mason	20,500	19,668	
Sub Total	$181,820	$174,536	
Builder + 10%	18,182	17,454	
Total	$200,002	$191,990	
Fair-tax 23%	0	$44,158	
Grand Total	$200,002	$236,148	
Price & % Increase	0	$36,146	+18%

As you can see in both examples the price increase is 18% it doesn't matter what figures you use, or what products you buy (Don't you just love math). The Fair-tax will bring along an 18% price increase on all goods and service. Incase some of you are wondering why the increase is not the 18.7% I've pounding down your throat, the answer is simple. I divided the IFS price increase by the IRS price of the house. The IFS price is less, remember when you take away 22% and add 23% the price is less. This gives us the IFS increase percentage over the original price of goods.

WHAT? Your a <u>Liar</u>! Your using the wrong figures, you have the service builders prices with the Fair-tax embedded in them. They don't pay the Fair-tax, only the builder charges the Fair-tax on the finished product. You have to remove those taxes, they don't pay the Fair-tax on the Trucks, Tools and Supplies they buy (Smell a Revenue Neutral problem here?) those taxes have to go.

OK, I'll take them out (Remember, you asked for it). The service builders didn't charge the builder the Fair-tax, although it was their end product. If they did the prices in the IFS column would be 23% higher, we're talking about the embedded Fair-tax they should have picked up along the way, buying Trucks, Tools, and

Supplies. But I'll take them out even though the Fair-tax is self-embedding and this will be impossible in the real world.

I won't do every figure individually, I'll just take the 23% off the service builders total, its the same thing.

	IRS	IFS
Cost of House	$181,820	$174,536
Embedded Fair-tax	0	-40,143
Sub Total	181,820	134,393
Builder's 10%	18,182	13,439
Sub Total	$202,002	$147,832
Fair-tax 23%	0	34,000
Total	$200,002	$181,832
% Diff. in Price	0	9% Less Then IRS
Embedded Tax 22%	44,000	0
Tax Collected	$44,000	$34,000 23% Less

You asked for it. The government collected $44,000 in embedded taxes from the IRS price, and only $34,000 from the Fair-tax and that's it, no more revenue to be made from the sale of the house. Not only does the government receive $44,000 it also collects Income Tax, Social Security Taxes, Medicare Tax, AMT., Death Tax, Capital Gains Tax, etc. you know the list. There is no way the Fair-tax on the house will be <u>Revenue Neutral</u> to the IRS taxes collected. To even come close the service builders will have to pay the Fair-tax on the Trucks, Tools, and Supplies they buy, after all they are the end products of other manufacturers. I'm sure the sale of these products were figured into the Revenue Neutral equation. When they do pay it, the Fair-tax cost will be included in the final price of their services. Thus raising the price of goods and services **18%**, we'll be dammed if they don't pay it, and dammed if they do (Talk about your double edged sword).

Remember I removed the embedded Fair-tax from the service builders in the amount of $40,143 (If that money is not paid at the time of purchase its gone forever and can <u>not</u> be retrieved) if they paid it, add that to the Fair-tax on the house, $44,158 and the government would collect **$84,301** on the construction and sale of the house, **$50,301** more than was collected on the house when the service builders didn't have to pay the Fair-tax. Do you think they'll have to pay it, or not? If its paid, the Fair-tax becomes embedded in all goods and services. Thus giving us an **18%** increase in prices . If its not paid, the hopes of the Fair-tax being Revenue Neutral goes right into the S&@##er (toilet).

AS I mentioned earlier the service builders did <u>not</u> charge the builder the Fair-tax on their services (Their finial end product). According to the Fair-tax they won't have too, but we're talking about a lot revenue to the Government, and the Fair-tax is desperate to become <u>Revenue Neutral.</u> So Just for the horror of it, lets look at the price of the house with the service builders charging the Fair-tax on their services.

	IRS	IFS	
Foundation	$14,250	$13,672	
Plumber	9,370	8,990	
Framer	18,900	18,133	
Roofer	38,000	36,457	
Drywall	20,000	19,188	
Electrician	12,500	11,993	
Painter	20,500	19,668	
Floors	10,000	9594	
Windows	17,800	17,173	
Mason	<u>20,500</u>	<u>19,668</u>	
Sub Total	$181,820	$174,536	
Service Fair-tax 23%	0	40,143	
Sub Total	181,820	214,679	
Builder + 10%	<u>18,182</u>	<u>21,468</u>	
Total	$200,002	$236,147	
Fair-tax 23%	0	$44,158	
Grand Total	$200,002	$290,460	
Price & % Increase	0	$90,458	+45.2%
Total Fair-tax Collected		**$84,301**	

Do you think the Government is going to settle for $44,158, or will the Service Builders be required to collect the Fair-tax on their services from the Builder?

Something else to make you feel good, lets say the service builders didn't charge the Fair-tax. If you had to rebuild your house for any reason, the price would be pretty close to the $290,460. The service builders would have to charge you the Fair-tax, because you are not building a new house for sale, your repairing an old one (It's old the day you bought it and paid the Fair-tax). The original cost of your house without the Fair-tax embedded in it was $181,832. About $108,628 more to replace your house, will you have the GAP Insurance (**G**rab **A**nkles and **P**ray) in place incase you have to rebuild completely.

Imports, such as Autos, Boats, Planes, Clothing, Coffee, Sugar etc (you know what they are). are all produced outside of this country, and will not have the benefit of having a 22% in place embedded tax removed. The cost of those items will go up **23%** under the Fair-tax. It will give new meaning to the words, <u>**Buy American.**</u> And buy they will, a month or so before the Fair-tax goes into effect Americans will buy everything in sight. With the price of domestic products going up **18%** and foreign products going up **23%** it will be an unstoppable catastrophe.

I'll bet the Black Market (Another story, won't get into it) will have a hand in this buying frenzy, we're not just talking Booze here, we're talking about **Everything!**

Something else related to the **18%** price increase, the Prebate Table. Currently the table is figured on 23%, when someone realizes that a 23% Fair-tax will only yield 18.7% revenue on the dollar, the table will or should be adjusted to 18.7%. Under the current table a family of four receives a monthly prebate check in the amount of **$506**, when the table is corrected the amount will be **$411**. With an **18%** increase in prices, we'll only have **.7%** for the taxes on the necessities of life. For a family of four that's a whopping **$2.88**, after you blow that, the rest comes out of your own pocket. Don't forget all the **New Taxes,** the Fair-tax will breed. (Chapter 10). **.7%** <u>**Big Deal!**</u> The prebate is designed for one reason and one reason only, to **Buy** support from the poor and lower income earners. Too bad someone just wised them up.

If it sounds to good to be true, it probably is.

They should spell it: <u>**Pre-bait**</u>.

FAIR-TAX VOTE
BUYING MADE EASY

Let's assume the Fair-tax is alive and well. It's working just like its supposed too. It's revenue neutral. Everybody is making more on their paychecks. There's no IRS, no compliance, or embedded taxes, and businesses are coming back to the U.S. faster than this book has been slammed, tossed, and stomped on. In other words, we'll throw out the previous eleven chapters, (I'll bet someone already has), and play to the Power of the Politician.

This is the scenario. It's a Presidential election year, the Presidential candidate for The Working Peoples Party is giving a campaign speech.

"Ladies and gentlemen I'm running for President to put an end to the UN-Fair-tax. This is a tax designed to keep the **Rich** in this country from paying their fair share of taxes! It's not fair that you the working people of this Nation living from paycheck to paycheck, pay the same tax as the Rich! When we go into a store and buy a our food we'll pay the same tax as the millionaire next to us. Now, I know there's no way to tell if someone making a purchase in a store is poor or a millionaire, so this is what I propose to do if you elect me President, and the other members of our party to Congress. I'll need the support of Congress to change things in our favor. As President I'll send a bill to our Congress that will:

One. Implement an immediate reduction of the 23% consumption-tax to 13%.

Two. Anyone earning five times over his or her poverty level will no longer receive a prebate check. After all why should we send a $500.00 check to a family of four that earns $200,000.00 a month.

Three. Any Registered voter (you must be a registered voter) who earns less money than their poverty level will receive a **Deserved Income Program** (DIP) check to bring them up to their poverty level. For example: A working mother with two children earning $18,000 a year has a poverty level of $ 23,000. Along with her prebate check of $ 441.00 a month. At the end of the year she'll will also receive a Deserved Income Program check in the amount of $5,000 to increase her income to the poverty level of $23,000. (That will get the homeless, and jobless out to voter registration, a single person's poverty level is $9,800). After all! <u>Why should the richest nation in the world</u>! <u>Have anyone in poverty</u>! Where will this money come from to fund the Deserved Income and the 10% reduction of the Fair-tax? As I said before, there will be millions of prebate checks not being issued to the people who earn over five times their poverty level, that's one way it will be covered. The other way, I'm going to propose a **Fair-Share-Tax** of 35% on all luxury goods! For example: A 35% tax on private aircraft and on the hanger space or tie downs to store it, also a 35% tax on LL100 (most of the people reading this don't know what LL 100 is and wouldn't care if it had a 60 % tax). Boats over 35 feet in length would have a 35% tax, also the dock rental for it. Dock side fuel purchases in excess of 100 gallons. Vehicles over $60,000 will have a Fair-Share-Tax of 35%. Also I'll discontinue the Fair-tax- on all vehicles under $25,000! Home purchases other than your **primary home** will have a 35% Fair-Share-Tax no matter if they are new or used. Primary homes under $200,000 will be Fair-tax **free**!

First class airline tickets, first class hotel accommodations, jewelry over a certain dollar amount will carry a 35% Fair-Share-Tax. I don't have time to list them all, but believe you me. I'll put a stop to it! The working people have had enough!

They put this Fair-tax on us. Now it's time to get this monkey off the backs of the working people, and put the Fair-Share-Tax where it should be, right in their greedy wallets! I'm looking forward to seeing all of you in Washington in January. Thank You."

WOW! Can you imagine this happening? I can. The Fair-tax is the biggest vote buying peace of legislation since the inception of kissing babies.

Lobbyists! There will be so many K street lobbyists in D.C. trying to keep their clients off the Fair-Share-Tax list, they'll need the abandoned IRS building just to hold them all.

If luxury items can be singled out for a higher tax other items could be also. For example. Crime, most people shot in this country are minorities and have no insurance, the cost of treatment and crime prevention could be offset by a 70% tax on hand gun sales, or all guns for that matter. The same could hold true for hunting and fishing or non energy efficient products. I don't dare to continue the list, the power the Fair-tax could yield is incalculable.

Let's face it, putting the budget of this nation solely on the consumption of products is far to dangerous. What happens if we go into a recession and inflation goes up? Most of us have been there, the first thing that happens is the price of goods go up, and consumption goes down, and now, <u>Revenue</u> with it. What's the answer? Raise the percentage of the Fair-tax to cover the <u>Reduction in Revenue</u>?

When the economy recovers, will the percentages be changed to the previous rates? What do you think?

Putting our Nation's budget on a consumption-tax is not even wishful thinking, it's not thinking at all, it's a pipe dream. The money needed just won't be there.

Remember just for the Fair-tax to break even with taxpayers (us) everyone of us will have to spend 100% of our income every year, rich or poor.

What about corporate business taxes? (I know they don't pay taxes, they just collect them from the consumer.) If the Fair-tax doesn't tax them where did that revenue go, and how do we get it back? Remember we are spending 100% of our money now just to "almost" keep up with lost Income and Payroll tax revenue!

The Deserved Income Program (DIP) mentioned in this speech, lets take a look at it. A college student will not only collect a prebate check of $188 a month, if he earns $7,500 a year while at school, he'll also receive a Deserved Income check in the amount of $2,300 (poverty level $9,800 - $7500 = $2,300). The same will hold true for the Jobless and the Homeless (as long as they're registered voters). With the Fair-tax budget for the prebate set at $560,000,000,000 (Five Hundred Sixty Billion), a half **Trillion Dollars** a year, and removing the high-income earners from the prebate program, and adding the Fair-Share-Tax there just might be plenty of money to accomplish this.

If this candidate won the Presidency and successfully implemented the Fair-Share-Tax, and the Deserved Income program, on what platform could any other party run on and **Win**? The Working Persons Party would remain in power forever.

One final thought on House Bill HR. 25.

"The Road to Hell is Paved With Good Intentions".

The flock has been sheered. See ya at the next **Rally.**

Review

1. We know that the $500 billion in compliance cost is not lost revenue, or lost opportunities, or a blow to our economy. The people who earned that money spend it just like we all do. Thus keeping it in our economy.

2. We learned that the Fair-tax is self-embedding. You can't stop it from happening, and you can't make it go away. Therefore all our products will have a 23% embedded tax in them, and will cost 18% more.

3. The Fair-tax is not revenue neutral. It only yields 18.7% tax revenue not 23%. It falls short 4.3% of expected earnings. People below the poverty level will pay Fair-tax compared to 0% IRS. People above the poverty level earning a five-figure income will see an **Increase** in taxes. People earning a six-figure incomes will see a **Reduction** in taxes. People earning seven figures or more will see a **Reduction** in taxes.

    Also in order for a $100.00 item to yield a $23.00 tax revenue it has to be marked up 30.0%. The Fair-tax uses the wrong math formula. Chapter Three touched on the problem of the devastatingly large Fair-tax bills on big-ticket items, and a possible way to circumnavigate a large portion of them, if not eliminating them altogether. What you can do with the $50,000 SUV you can do with just about any big ticket item.

4. In order to buy a $246,000 house you have to finance the $46,000 Fair-tax separately from the mortgage of $200,000. Or pay the Fair-tax up front. The tax has no value and builds no equity, it's gone. Same for vehicles, boats, planes, etc. GAP Insurance, if you had to rebuild a house the Fair-tax would have to be paid again and then some.

5. Instead of American business coming home, more of them my leave to stay competitive, because of the self embedding Fair-tax.

6. The underground and off shore economy are being taxed right now. As we learned when they spend their money, the 22% embedded tax already in place taxes them. In fact they will receive a 1.3% reduction in tax if the Fair-tax is passed. The same holds true for Illegal Emigrants.

7. Employers will not pass on to the employee the payroll taxes paid by the employee or himself 7.6% each or 15.2% total. The employer will keep it. Also by changing

job titles he will be able to keep the income withholding tax the employees paid.

8. When you take 22% embedded tax away from an item, and add 23% Fair-tax to it gets cheaper. Everyone in this country will receive a prebate check. Including the Jobless. Homeless, and collage students. They are consumers too, and pay the Fair-tax. It will cost over a half **$Trillion** a year to fund the prebate program. It will also Raise our National Deficit 307%.

9. Social Security will be paid to everyone. Most of which will be the maximum benefits. The cost of compliance will not disappear. We'll have to send in payroll reports, personal income reports, set up bank accounts for collected Fair-tax monies. Checks and records to send to the IFS, Reports on who paid and did not pay the Fair-tax

10. We'll get hit with so many **New Taxes** it will use up the Prebate check. Leaving us with a 18% increase in the price of goods and services. The New Taxes will be devastating to the lower income earners. 23% tax on the Internet, Phone. Gas, Electric, Water, Sewer just to name a few. All services will have a 23% tax on them.

11. The Fair-tax must be paid by all business for the Fair-tax too have any hope of being Revenue Neutral or coming close to it. Imports will have a 23% price increase. The cost to rebuild a house will be considerable more, because the Fair-tax will have to be paid to the service providers. Insurance will have to be purchased to cover the extra cost over the original price.

12. The Fair-tax is one of the biggest vote buying peace's of legislation. With the Fair-**Share**-Tax, lobbyists will remain alive and well. What possible platform could someone from another party run on and <u>WIN</u>, when the Working Person Party implements the Fair-Share-Tax and the Deserved Income Program. Putting our Nations budget solely on a consumption-tax is not only dangerous, It's foolhardy. The Deserved Income Program (DIP) will guarantee every person will earn at least the amount of their personal poverty level, in addition to their prebate checks.

Back of the Book

2006 Federal Poverty Level Guidelines

Family Unit	Federal 2006 FPL Annual Income	Federal 2006 FPL Monthly Income
1	$9,800	$817
2	13,200	$1,100
3	16,600	$1,383
4	20,000	$1,667
5	23,400	$1,950
6	26,800	$2,233
7	30,200	$2,517
8	33,600	$2,800
For each additional person add	$3,400	$283

Annual income based on 2006 Federal Poverty Level (FPL) Guidelines

Family Size	251%	351%	451%	551%	651%	751%	851%	1001%
1	24,598	34,398	44,198	53,998	63,798	73,598	83,398	98,098
2	33,132	48,332	59,532	72,732	85,932	99,132	112,332	132,132
3	41,666	58,266	74,866	91,466	108,066	124,666	141,266	166,166
4	50,200	70,200	90,200	110,200	130,200	150,200	170,200	200,200
5	58,734	82,134	105,534	128,934	152,334	175,734	199,134	234,234
6	67,268	94,068	120,868	147,668	174,468	201,268	228,068	268,268
7	75,802	106,002	136,202	166,402	196,602	226,802	257,002	302,302
8	84,336	117,936	151,536	185,136	218,736	252336	285,936	336,336

People MapStats	Florida	USA
Population. 2005 estimate	17.789,864	**296,410.404**
Population, percent change, April 1, 2000 to July 1. 2005	11.3%	5.3%
7 Population, change. April 1, 2000 to July 1, 2005	1.807.040	14,985,802
Population, 2000	15,982,378	281.421,906
? Persons under 5 years old, 2005	1,118,829	20,303,724
Persons under 5 years old, percent. 2005	6.3%	6.8%
Persons under 18 years old, 2005	4,067,877	**73,469,984**
? Persons under 18 years old, percent, 2005	229%	24.8%
Persons 65 years old and over, percent, 2005	16.8%	12.4%
? Persons 65 years old and over, 2005	2,993,160	36.790,113
Female persons, percent, 2005	51.0%	50 7%

Summary of Taxpayers

Taxpayer #1

Income	18,000
Social Security	1,116
Medicare	216
Total	16,668
Tax Paid	+4,680
Net Income	21,348
% Tax Paid	-11.8 or +3,348

IFS

Income	18,000
Prebate	3,816
Total Income	21,816
Income Spent	21,816
Fair-tax Paid 23%	5,017

% Tax Paid to IRS -11.8   % Tax Paid to IFS +23.0

Total Tax Collected by IRS Including Employer and Employee Payroll Taxes   **Total Fair-tax Collected**

Income Tax	+4,680
Employee Payroll	1,332
Employer Payroll	1,332

Total Tax Collected	-2,016	Fair-tax	5,017
Plus or Minus (+ OR-)	REVENUE NEUTRAL	Plus +5,017	

Summary of Taxpayers

Taxpayer #2

Income	48,000
Social Security	-2976
Medicare	-696
Total	44,328
Tax Paid	6799
Net Income	37,529
% Tax Paid	21.8 or 10,471

IFS

Income	48,000
Prebate	2,254
Total Income	50254
Income Spent	42,754
Fair-tax Paid 23%	9,833

% Tax Paid to IRS 21.8   % Tax Paid to IFS 23.0

Total Tax Collected by IRS Including Employer and Employee Payroll Taxes   **Total Fair-tax Collected**

Income Tax	6,799
Employee Payroll	3,672
Employer Payroll	3,672

Total Tax Collected	14,143	Fair-tax	9,833

Plus or Minus (+ OR-)   REVENUE NEUTRAL   Minus –4,310

Summary of Taxpayers

Taxpayer #3

Income	48,000
Social Security	2,976
Medicare	696
Total	44,328
Tax Paid	1,054
Net Income	43,274
% Tax Paid	9.8 or 4,726

IFS

Income	48,000
Prebate	6,072
Total Income	54,072
Income Spent	50,072
Fair-tax Paid 23%	12,436

% Tax Paid to IRS 9.8   % Tax Paid to IFS 23.0

Total Tax Collected by IRS Including Employer and Employee Payroll Taxes   **Total Fair-tax Collected**

Income Tax	1,054
Employee Payroll	3,672
Employer Payroll	3,672

Total Tax Collected	8,398	**Fair-tax**	12,436
Plus or Minus (+ OR -)	REVENUE NEUTRAL	Plus +4,038	

Summary of Taxpayers

Taxpayer # 4

Income	**480,000**
Social Security	**5,456**
Medicare	**6,960**
Total	**467,584**
Tax Paid	**138,563**
Net Income	**329,021**
% Tax Paid	**31.4 or 150,979**

IFS

Income	**480,000**
Prebate	**6,072**
Total Income	**486,072**
Income Spent	**364,554**
Fair-tax Paid 23%	**83,847**

% Tax Paid to IRS 31.4   **% Tax Paid to IFS 23.0**

Total Tax Collected by IRS Including Employer and Employee Payroll Taxes   **Total Fair-tax Collected**

Income Tax	**138,563**
Employee Payroll	**12,416**
Employer Payroll	**12,416**

Total Tax Collected	**163,395**	**Fair-tax**	**83,847**
Plus or Minus (+ OR-)	**REVENUE NEUTRAL**	**Minus –79,548**	

Summary of Taxpayers

Taxpayer # 5

Income	4,800,000
Social Security	5456
Medicare	69,600
Total	4,724,944
Tax Paid	1,650,563
Net Income	3,725,619
% Tax Paid	35.9 or 1,725,619

IFS

Income	4,800,000
Prebate	6,072
Total Income	4,806,072
Income Spent	2,403,036
Fair-tax Paid 23%	552,698

% Tax Paid to IRS 35.9   **% Tax Paid to IFS 23.0**

Total Tax Collected by IRS Including Employer and Employee Payroll Taxes   **Total Fair-tax Collected**

Income Tax	1,650,563		
Employee Payroll	75,056		
Employer Payroll	75,056		
Total Tax Collected	1,800,675	**Fair-tax**	552,698
Plus or Minus (+ OR-)	REVENUE NEUTRAL	Minus –1,247,977	

PERCENT PLUS or MINUS CHANGE IN TAXES PAID PAYROLL TAXES INCLUDED

TAX PAYER	PMT. IRS	%	PMT. IFS	%	%+OR-
#1	3,348	-11.8	5,017	23.0	+34.8
#2	10,471	21.8	9,833	23.0	+1.2
#3	4,726	9.8	12,436	23.0	+13.2
#4	150,979	31.4	83,847	23.0	-8.4
#5	1,725,619	35.9	552,698	23.0	-12.9
TOTAL	1,888,447	100.00	663,831		-64.8

Taxpayer #1 page 1

Form 1040 — U.S. Individual Income Tax Return 2006

Department of the Treasury—Internal Revenue Service (99)
For the year Jan. 1–Dec. 31, 2006, or other tax year beginning , 2006, ending , 20
OMB No. 1545-0074
IRS Use Only—Do not write or staple in this space.

Label (See instructions on page 16.) Use the IRS label. Otherwise, please print or type.

- Your first name and initial: **WINDY**
- Last name: **H**
- Your social security number: **111 11 111**
- If a joint return, spouse's first name and initial: (blank)
- Last name: (blank)
- Spouse's social security number: (blank)
- Home address (number and street): (blank) — Apt. no.: (blank)
- City, town or post office, state, and ZIP code: **APOPKA, FL 32712**

Presidential Election Campaign ▶ Check here if you, or your spouse if filing jointly, want $3 to go to this fund (see page 16) ▶ ☐ You ☐ Spouse

Filing Status — Check only one box.

1. ☑ Single
2. ☐ Married filing jointly (even if only one had income)
3. ☐ Married filing separately. Enter spouse's SSN above and full name here. ▶
4. ☐ Head of household (with qualifying person). (See page 17.) If the qualifying person is a child but not your dependent, enter this child's name here. ▶
5. ☐ Qualifying widow(er) with dependent child (see page 17)

Exemptions

6a ☑ Yourself. If someone can claim you as a dependent, do not check box 6a
6b ☐ Spouse

6c Dependents:

(1) First name Last name	(2) Dependent's social security number	(3) Dependent's relationship to you	(4) ✓ if qualifying child for child tax credit (see page 19)
SHERRY H	222 22 2222	daughter	✓
DONALD H	333 33 3333	son	✓

- Boxes checked on 6a and 6b: **1**
- No. of children on 6c who: lived with you: **2**; did not live with you due to divorce or separation (see page 20): (blank)
- Dependents on 6c not entered above: (blank)
- Add numbers on lines above ▶ **3**

Income

Attach Form(s) W-2 here. Also attach Forms W-2G and 1099-R if tax was withheld.

If you did not get a W-2, see page 23.

Enclose, but do not attach, any payment. Also, please use Form 1040-V.

7. Wages, salaries, tips, etc. Attach Form(s) W-2 .... **18,000**
8a. Taxable interest. Attach Schedule B if required ....
8b. Tax-exempt interest. Do not include on line 8a ....
9a. Ordinary dividends. Attach Schedule B if required ....
9b. Qualified dividends (see page 23) ....
10. Taxable refunds, credits, or offsets of state and local income taxes (see page 24)
11. Alimony received
12. Business income or (loss). Attach Schedule C or C-EZ
13. Capital gain or (loss). Attach Schedule D if required. If not required, check here ▶ ☐
14. Other gains or (losses). Attach Form 4797
15a. IRA distributions .... 15b Taxable amount (see page 25)
16a. Pensions and annuities .... 16b Taxable amount (see page 26)
17. Rental real estate, royalties, partnerships, S corporations, trusts, etc. Attach Schedule E
18. Farm income or (loss). Attach Schedule F
19. Unemployment compensation
20a. Social security benefits .... 20b Taxable amount (see page 27)
21. Other income. List type and amount (see page 29)
22. Add the amounts in the far right column for lines 7 through 21. This is your **total income** ▶ **18,000**

Adjusted Gross Income

23. Archer MSA deduction. Attach Form 8853
24. Certain business expenses of reservists, performing artists, and fee-basis government officials. Attach Form 2106 or 2106-EZ
25. Health savings account deduction. Attach Form 8889
26. Moving expenses. Attach Form 3903
27. One-half of self-employment tax. Attach Schedule SE
28. Self-employed SEP, SIMPLE, and qualified plans
29. Self-employed health insurance deduction (see page 29)
30. Penalty on early withdrawal of savings
31a. Alimony paid b Recipient's SSN ▶
32. IRA deduction (see page 31)
33. Student loan interest deduction (see page 33)
34. Jury duty pay you gave to your employer
35. Domestic production activities deduction. Attach Form 8903
36. Add lines 23 through 31a and 32 through 35
37. Subtract line 36 from line 22. This is your **adjusted gross income** ▶ **18,000**

For Disclosure, Privacy Act, and Paperwork Reduction Act Notice, see page 80. Cat. No. 11320B Form **1040** (2006)

Taxpayer #1 page 2

Form 1040 (2006) — Page 2

Tax and Credits

- **38** Amount from line 37 (adjusted gross income) — **38** 18,000
- **39a** Check if: ☐ You were born before January 2, 1942, ☐ Blind. ☐ Spouse was born before January 2, 1942, ☐ Blind. Total boxes checked ▶ 39a
- **b** If your spouse itemizes on a separate return or you were a dual-status alien, see page 34 and check here ▶ 39b ☐
- **40** Itemized deductions (from Schedule A) or your standard deduction (see left margin) — **40** 7,300
- **41** Subtract line 40 from line 38 — **41** 10,700
- **42** If line 38 is over $112,875, or you provided housing to a person displaced by Hurricane Katrina, see page 36. Otherwise, multiply $3,300 by the total number of exemptions claimed on line 6d — **42** 9,600
- **43** Taxable income. Subtract line 42 from line 41. If line 42 is more than line 41, enter -0- — **43** 1,100
- **44** Tax (see page 36). Check if any tax is from: a ☐ Form(s) 8814 b ☐ Form 4972 — **44** 111
- **45** Alternative minimum tax (see page 39). Attach Form 6251 — **45**
- **46** Add lines 44 and 45 ▶ **46** 111
- **47** Foreign tax credit. Attach Form 1116 if required — 47
- **48** Credit for child and dependent care expenses. Attach Form 2441 — 48
- **49** Credit for the elderly or the disabled. Attach Schedule R — 49
- **50** Education credits. Attach Form 8863 — 50
- **51** Retirement savings contributions credit. Attach Form 8880 — 51
- **52** Residential energy credits. Attach Form 5695 — 52 111
- **53** Child tax credit (see page 42). Attach Form 8901 if required — 53
- **54** Credits from: a ☐ Form 8396 b ☐ Form 8839 c ☐ Form 8859 — 54
- **55** Other credits: a ☐ Form 3800 b ☐ Form 8801 c ☐ Form — 55
- **56** Add lines 47 through 55. These are your total credits — **56** 111
- **57** Subtract line 56 from line 46. If line 56 is more than line 46, enter -0- ▶ **57**

Standard Deduction for—
- People who checked any box on line 39a or 39b **or** who can be claimed as a dependent, see page 34.
- All others:
  - Single or Married filing separately, $5,150
  - Married filing jointly or Qualifying widow(er), $10,300
  - Head of household, $7,550

Other Taxes

- **58** Self-employment tax. Attach Schedule SE — **58**
- **59** Social security and Medicare tax on tip income not reported to employer. Attach Form 4137 — **59**
- **60** Additional tax on IRAs, other qualified retirement plans, etc. Attach Form 5329 if required — **60**
- **61** Advance earned income credit payments from Form(s) W-2, box 9 — **61**
- **62** Household employment taxes. Attach Schedule H — **62**
- **63** Add lines 57 through 62. This is your total tax ▶ **63**

Payments

- **64** Federal income tax withheld from Forms W-2 and 1099 — 64
- **65** 2006 estimated tax payments and amount applied from 2005 return — 65
- **66a** Earned income credit (EIC) — 66a 3,630
- **b** Nontaxable combat pay election ▶ 66b
- **67** Excess social security and tier 1 RRTA tax withheld (see page 60) — 67
- **68** Additional child tax credit. Attach Form 8812 — 68 1,050
- **69** Amount paid with request for extension to file (see page 60) — 69
- **70** Payments from: a ☐ Form 2439 b ☐ Form 4136 c ☐ Form 8885 — 70
- **71** Credit for federal telephone excise tax paid. Attach Form 8913 if required — 71
- **72** Add lines 64, 65, 66a, and 67 through 71. These are your total payments ▶ **72** 4,580

If you have a qualifying child, attach Schedule EIC.

Refund

- **73** If line 72 is more than line 63, subtract line 63 from line 72. This is the amount you overpaid — **73** 4,680
- **74a** Amount of line 73 you want refunded to you. If Form 8888 is attached, check here ▶ ☐ — **74a** 4,680
- **b** Routing number: X X X X X X X X X ▶ c Type: ☐ Checking ☐ Savings
- **d** Account number: X X X X X X X X X X X X X X X X X
- **75** Amount of line 73 you want applied to your 2007 estimated tax ▶ 75

Direct deposit? See page 61 and fill in 74b, 74c, and 74d, or Form 8888.

Amount You Owe

- **76** Amount you owe. Subtract line 72 from line 63. For details on how to pay, see page 62 ▶ **76**
- **77** Estimated tax penalty (see page 62) — 77

Third Party Designee

Do you want to allow another person to discuss this return with the IRS (see page 63)? ☐ Yes. Complete the following. ☑ No

Designee's name ▶   Phone no. (   )   Personal identification number (PIN) ▶

Sign Here

Under penalties of perjury, I declare that I have examined this return and accompanying schedules and statements, and to the best of my knowledge and belief, they are true, correct, and complete. Declaration of preparer (other than taxpayer) is based on all information of which preparer has any knowledge.

Your signature | Date | Your occupation | Daytime phone number ( )

Spouse's signature. If a joint return, both must sign. | Date | Spouse's occupation

Joint return? See page 17. Keep a copy for your records.

Paid Preparer's Use Only

Preparer's signature ▶ | Date | Check if self-employed ☐ | Preparer's SSN or PTIN

Firm's name (or yours if self-employed), address, and ZIP code ▶ | EIN | Phone no. (   )

Form **1040** (2006)

Taxpayer #1 page 3

SCHEDULE EIC
(Form 1040A or 1040)

Department of the Treasury
Internal Revenue Service (99)

Earned Income Credit
Qualifying Child Information

Complete and attach to Form 1040A or 1040 only if you have a qualifying child.

OMB No. 1545-0074

2006

Attachment Sequence No. **43**

Name(s) shown on return	Your social security number
WINDY H	111 : 11 : 1111

Before you begin: See the instructions for Form 1040A, lines 40a and 40b, or Form 1040, lines 66a and 66b, to make sure that **(a)** you can take the EIC, and **(b)** you have a qualifying child.

- If you take the EIC even though you are not eligible, you may not be allowed to take the credit for up to 10 years. See back of schedule for details.
- It will take us longer to process your return and issue your refund if you do not fill in all lines that apply for each qualifying child.
- Be sure the child's name on line 1 and social security number (SSN) on line 2 agree with the child's social security card. Otherwise, at the time we process your return, we may reduce or disallow your EIC. If the name or SSN on the child's social security card is not correct, call the Social Security Administration at 1-800-772-1213.

Qualifying Child Information	Child 1	Child 2
1 Child's name If you have more than two qualifying children, you only have to list two to get the maximum credit.	First name: SHERRY H Last name:	First name: DONALD H Last name:
2 Child's SSN The child must have an SSN as defined on page 43 of the Form 1040A instructions or page 49 of the Form 1040 instructions unless the child was born and died in 2006. If your child was born and died in 2006 and did not have an SSN, enter "Died" on this line and attach a copy of the child's birth certificate.	222 : 22 : 2222	333 : 33 : 3333
3 Child's year of birth	Year 2 0 0 0 *If born after 1987, skip lines 4a and 4b; go to line 5.*	Year 2 0 0 4 *If born after 1987, skip lines 4a and 4b; go to line 5.*
4 If the child was born before 1988— **a** Was the child under age 24 at the end of 2006 and a student?	☐ Yes. *Go to line 5.* ☑ No. *Continue.*	☐ Yes. *Go to line 5.* ☑ No. *Continue.*
b Was the child permanently and totally disabled during any part of 2006?	☐ Yes. *Continue.* ☐ No. *The child is not a qualifying child.*	☐ Yes. *Continue.* ☐ No. *The child is not a qualifying child.*
5 Child's relationship to you (for example, son, daughter, grandchild, niece, nephew, foster child, etc.)	DAUGHTER	SON
6 Number of months child lived with you in the United States during 2006 • If the child lived with you for more than half of 2006 but less than 7 months, enter "7." • If the child was born or died in 2006 and your home was the child's home for the entire time he or she was alive during 2006, enter "12."	12 months *Do not enter more than 12 months.*	12 months *Do not enter more than 12 months.*

TIP You may also be able to take the additional child tax credit if your child **(a)** was under age 17 at the end of 2006, **and (b)** is a U.S. citizen or resident alien. For more details, see the instructions for line 41 of Form 1040A or line 68 of Form 1040.

For Paperwork Reduction Act Notice, see Form 1040A or 1040 instructions.   Cat. No. 13339M   Schedule EIC (Form 1040A or 1040) 2006

Taxpayer #2 page 1

Form 1040 — U.S. Individual Income Tax Return 2006

Department of the Treasury—Internal Revenue Service
For the year Jan. 1–Dec. 31, 2006, or other tax year beginning , 2006, ending , 20
OMB No. 1545-0074

Label (See instructions on page 16.) Use the IRS label. Otherwise, please print or type.

Your first name and initial: WINDEL
Last name: H
Home address (number and street). If you have a P.O. box, see page 16.
City, town or post office, state, and ZIP code. APOPKA, FL 32712
Your social security number: 111 11 111

Presidential Election Campaign ▶ Check here if you, or your spouse if filing jointly, want $3 to go to this fund (see page 16) ▶ ☐ You ☐ Spouse

Filing Status — Check only one box.
1. ☐ Single
2. ☐ Married filing jointly (even if only one had income)
3. ☐ Married filing separately. Enter spouse's SSN above and full name here. ▶
4. ☐ Head of household (with qualifying person). (See page 17.) If the qualifying person is a child but not your dependent, enter this child's name here. ▶
5. ☐ Qualifying widow(er) with dependent child (see page 17)

Exemptions
- 6a ☐ Yourself. If someone can claim you as a dependent, do not check box 6a
- b ☐ Spouse
- c Dependents:

Income
- 7 Wages, salaries, tips, etc. Attach Form(s) W-2 7   48,000
- 8a Taxable interest. Attach Schedule B if required 8a
- b Tax-exempt interest. Do not include on line 8a ... 8b
- 9a Ordinary dividends. Attach Schedule B if required 9a
- b Qualified dividends (see page 23) ... 9b
- 10 Taxable refunds, credits, or offsets of state and local income taxes (see page 24) . 10
- 11 Alimony received 11
- 12 Business income or (loss). Attach Schedule C or C-EZ 12
- 13 Capital gain or (loss). Attach Schedule D if required. If not required, check here ▶ ☐ 13
- 14 Other gains or (losses). Attach Form 4797 14
- 15a IRA distributions . 15a   b Taxable amount (see page 25) 15b
- 16a Pensions and annuities 16a   b Taxable amount (see page 26) 16b
- 17 Rental real estate, royalties, partnerships, S corporations, trusts, etc. Attach Schedule E . 17
- 18 Farm income or (loss). Attach Schedule F 18
- 19 Unemployment compensation 19
- 20a Social security benefits . 20a   b Taxable amount (see page 27) 20b
- 21 Other income. List type and amount (see page 29) _____ 21
- 22 Add the amounts in the far right column for lines 7 through 21. This is your **total income** ▶ 22   48,000

Adjusted Gross Income
- 23 Archer MSA deduction. Attach Form 8853 . 23
- 24 Certain business expenses of reservists, performing artists, and fee-basis government officials. Attach Form 2106 or 2106-EZ 24
- 25 Health savings account deduction. Attach Form 8889 . 25
- 26 Moving expenses. Attach Form 3903 . 26
- 27 One-half of self-employment tax. Attach Schedule SE . 27
- 28 Self-employed SEP, SIMPLE, and qualified plans . 28
- 29 Self-employed health insurance deduction (see page 29) 29
- 30 Penalty on early withdrawal of savings . 30
- 31a Alimony paid   b Recipient's SSN ▶ _____ 31a
- 32 IRA deduction (see page 31) . 32
- 33 Student loan interest deduction (see page 33) . 33
- 34 Jury duty pay you gave to your employer . 34
- 35 Domestic production activities deduction. Attach Form 8903 . 35
- 36 Add lines 23 through 31a and 32 through 35 36
- 37 Subtract line 36 from line 22. This is your **adjusted gross income** ▶ 37   48,000

For Disclosure, Privacy Act, and Paperwork Reduction Act Notice, see page 80. Cat. No. 11320B Form 1040 (2006)

Taxpayer #2 page 2

Form 1040 (2006) — Page 2

Tax and Credits

Standard Deduction for—
- People who checked any box on line 39a or 39b or who can be claimed as a dependent, see page 34.
- All others:
  Single or Married filing separately, $5,150
  Married filing jointly or Qualifying widow(er), $10,300
  Head of household, $7,550

Line	Description	Amount
38	Amount from line 37 (adjusted gross income)	48,000
39a	Check if: You were born before January 2, 1942, ☐ Blind. Spouse was born before January 2, 1942, ☐ Blind. Total boxes checked ▶ 39a	
39b	If your spouse itemizes on a separate return or you were a dual-status alien, see page 34 and check here ▶ 39b ☐	
40	Itemized deductions (from Schedule A) or your standard deduction (see left margin)	5,000
41	Subtract line 40 from line 38	43,000
42	If line 38 is over $112,875, or you provided housing to a person displaced by Hurricane Katrina, see page 36. Otherwise, multiply $3,300 by the total number of exemptions claimed on line 6d	3,200
43	Taxable income. Subtract line 42 from line 41. If line 42 is more than line 41, enter -0-	39,800
44	Tax (see page 36). Check if any tax is from: a ☐ Form(s) 8814 b ☐ Form 4972	6,621
45	Alternative minimum tax (see page 39). Attach Form 6251	
46	Add lines 44 and 45	6,621
47	Foreign tax credit. Attach Form 1116 if required	
48	Credit for child and dependent care expenses. Attach Form 2441	
49	Credit for the elderly or the disabled. Attach Schedule R	
50	Education credits. Attach Form 8863	
51	Retirement savings contributions credit. Attach Form 8880	
52	Residential energy credits. Attach Form 5695	
53	Child tax credit (see page 42). Attach Form 8901 if required	
54	Credits from: a ☐ Form 8396 b ☐ Form 8839 c ☐ Form 8859	
55	Other credits: a ☐ Form 3800 b ☐ Form 8801 c ☐ Form ___	
56	Add lines 47 through 55. These are your total credits	
57	Subtract line 56 from line 46. If line 56 is more than line 46, enter -0-	6,621

Other Taxes

Line	Description	Amount
58	Self-employment tax. Attach Schedule SE	
59	Social security and Medicare tax on tip income not reported to employer. Attach Form 4137	
60	Additional tax on IRAs, other qualified retirement plans, etc. Attach Form 5329 if required	
61	Advance earned income credit payments from Form(s) W-2, box 9	
62	Household employment taxes. Attach Schedule H	
63	Add lines 57 through 62. This is your total tax	6,621

Payments

If you have a qualifying child, attach Schedule EIC.

Line	Description	Amount
64	Federal income tax withheld from Forms W-2 and 1099	
65	2006 estimated tax payments and amount applied from 2005 return	
66a	Earned income credit (EIC)	
66b	Nontaxable combat pay election ▶	
67	Excess social security and tier 1 RRTA tax withheld (see page 60)	
68	Additional child tax credit. Attach Form 8812	
69	Amount paid with request for extension to file (see page 60)	
70	Payments from: a ☐ Form 2439 b ☐ Form 4136 c ☐ Form 8885	
71	Credit for federal telephone excise tax paid. Attach Form 8913 if required	
72	Add lines 64, 65, 66a, and 67 through 71. These are your total payments	

Refund

Direct deposit? See page 61 and fill in 74b, 74c, and 74d, or Form 8888.

Line	Description	Amount
73	If line 72 is more than line 63, subtract line 63 from line 72. This is the amount you overpaid	
74a	Amount of line 73 you want refunded to you. If Form 8888 is attached, check here ▶ ☐	
74b	Routing number: X X X X X X X X X ▶ c Type: ☐ Checking ☐ Savings	
74d	Account number: X X X X X X X X X X X X X X X X X	
75	Amount of line 73 you want applied to your 2007 estimated tax ▶	

Amount You Owe

Line	Description	Amount
76	Amount you owe. Subtract line 72 from line 63. For details on how to pay, see page 62 ▶	6,799
77	Estimated tax penalty (see page 62)	

Third Party Designee

Do you want to allow another person to discuss this return with the IRS (see page 63)? ☐ Yes. Complete the following. ✓ No

Designee's name ___ Phone no. ( ) Personal identification number (PIN) ___

Sign Here

Under penalties of perjury, I declare that I have examined this return and accompanying schedules and statements, and to the best of my knowledge and belief, they are true, correct, and complete. Declaration of preparer (other than taxpayer) is based on all information of which preparer has any knowledge.

Joint return? See page 17. Keep a copy for your records.

Your signature ___ Date ___ Your occupation ___ Daytime phone number ( )

Spouse's signature. If a joint return, both must sign. Date ___ Spouse's occupation ___

Paid Preparer's Use Only

Preparer's signature ___ Date ___ Check if self-employed ☐ Preparer's SSN or PTIN ___

Firm's name (or yours if self-employed), address, and ZIP code ___ EIN ___ Phone no. ( )

Form 1040 (2006)

Taxpayer #3 page 1

Form 1040 — U.S. Individual Income Tax Return 2006

Department of the Treasury—Internal Revenue Service (99) — IRS Use Only—Do not write or staple in this space.

For the year Jan. 1–Dec. 31, 2006, or other tax year beginning , 2006, ending , 20

OMB No. 1545-0074

Label (See instructions on page 16.) Use the IRS label. Otherwise, please print or type.

- Your first name and initial: **WINDEL**
- Last name: **H**
- Your social security number: **111 11 111**
- If a joint return, spouse's first name and initial: **WINDY**
- Last name: **H**
- Spouse's social security number: **444 44 4444**
- Home address (number and street). If you have a P.O. box, see page 16. Apt. no.
- City, town or post office, state, and ZIP code. **APOPKA, FL 32712**

You **must** enter your SSN(s) above.

Presidential Election Campaign ▶ Check here if you, or your spouse if filing jointly, want $3 to go to this fund (see page 16) ▶ ☐ You ☐ Spouse

Checking a box below will not change your tax or refund.

Filing Status

Check only one box.

1. ☐ Single
2. ☑ Married filing jointly (even if only one had income)
3. ☐ Married filing separately. Enter spouse's SSN above and full name here. ▶
4. ☐ Head of household (with qualifying person). (See page 17.) If the qualifying person is a child but not your dependent, enter this child's name here. ▶
5. ☐ Qualifying widow(er) with dependent child (see page 17)

Exemptions

- 6a ☑ **Yourself.** If someone can claim you as a dependent, **do not** check box 6a
- b ☑ **Spouse**
- c Dependents:

(1) First name Last name	(2) Dependent's social security number	(3) Dependent's relationship to you	(4) ☑ if qualifying child for child tax credit (see page 19)
SHERRY H	222 22 2222	daughter	☑
DONALD H	333 33 3333	son	☑
			☐
			☐

If more than four dependents, see page 19.

- Boxes checked on 6a and 6b: **2**
- No. of children on 6c who:
  - lived with you: **2**
  - did not live with you due to divorce or separation (see page 20)
- Dependents on 6c not entered above
- Add numbers on lines above ▶ **4**

d Total number of exemptions claimed

Income

Attach Form(s) W-2 here. Also attach Forms W-2G and 1099-R if tax was withheld.

If you did not get a W-2, see page 23.

Enclose, but do not attach, any payment. Also, please use Form 1040-V.

Line	Description	Amount
7	Wages, salaries, tips, etc. Attach Form(s) W-2	48,000
8a	Taxable interest. Attach Schedule B if required	
8b	Tax-exempt interest. **Do not** include on line 8a	
9a	Ordinary dividends. Attach Schedule B if required	
9b	Qualified dividends (see page 23)	
10	Taxable refunds, credits, or offsets of state and local income taxes (see page 24)	
11	Alimony received	
12	Business income or (loss). Attach Schedule C or C-EZ	
13	Capital gain or (loss). Attach Schedule D if required. If not required, check here ▶ ☐	
14	Other gains or (losses). Attach Form 4797	
15a	IRA distributions b Taxable amount (see page 25)	15b
16a	Pensions and annuities b Taxable amount (see page 26)	16b
17	Rental real estate, royalties, partnerships, S corporations, trusts, etc. Attach Schedule E	
18	Farm income or (loss). Attach Schedule F	
19	Unemployment compensation	
20a	Social security benefits b Taxable amount (see page 27)	20b
21	Other income. List type and amount (see page 29)	
22	Add the amounts in the far right column for lines 7 through 21. This is your **total income** ▶	48,000

Adjusted Gross Income

Line	Description	Amount
23	Archer MSA deduction. Attach Form 8853	
24	Certain business expenses of reservists, performing artists, and fee-basis government officials. Attach Form 2106 or 2106-EZ	
25	Health savings account deduction. Attach Form 8889	
26	Moving expenses. Attach Form 3903	
27	One-half of self-employment tax. Attach Schedule SE	
28	Self-employed SEP, SIMPLE, and qualified plans	
29	Self-employed health insurance deduction (see page 29)	
30	Penalty on early withdrawal of savings	
31a	Alimony paid b Recipient's SSN ▶	
32	IRA deduction (see page 31)	
33	Student loan interest deduction (see page 33)	
34	Jury duty pay you gave to your employer	
35	Domestic production activities deduction. Attach Form 8903	
36	Add lines 23 through 31a and 32 through 35	
37	Subtract line 36 from line 22. This is your **adjusted gross income** ▶	48,000

For Disclosure, Privacy Act, and Paperwork Reduction Act Notice, see page 80.   Cat. No. 11320B   Form **1040** (2006)

Taxpayer #3 page 2

Form 1040 (2006)

Tax and Credits

Line	Description	Amount
38	Amount from line 37 (adjusted gross income)	48,000
39a	Check if: You were born before January 2, 1942, ☐ Blind. Spouse was born before January 2, 1942, ☐ Blind. Total boxes checked ▶ 39a	
39b	If your spouse itemizes on a separate return or you were a dual-status alien, see page 34 and check here ▶ 39b ☐	
40	Itemized deductions (from Schedule A) or your standard deduction (see left margin)	10,000
41	Subtract line 40 from line 38	38,000
42	If line 38 is over $112,875, or you provided housing to a person displaced by Hurricane Katrina, see page 36. Otherwise, multiply $3,300 by the total number of exemptions claimed on line 6d	12,800
43	Taxable income. Subtract line 42 from line 41. If line 42 is more than line 41, enter -0-	25,200
44	Tax (see page 36). Check if any tax is from: a ☐ Form(s) 8814 b ☐ Form 4972	3,054
45	Alternative minimum tax (see page 39). Attach Form 6251	
46	Add lines 44 and 45 ▶	3,054
47	Foreign tax credit. Attach Form 1116 if required	
48	Credit for child and dependent care expenses. Attach Form 2441	
49	Credit for the elderly or the disabled. Attach Schedule R	
50	Education credits. Attach Form 8863	
51	Retirement savings contributions credit. Attach Form 8880	
52	Residential energy credits. Attach Form 5695	2,000
53	Child tax credit (see page 42). Attach Form 8901 if required	
54	Credits from: a ☐ Form 8396 b ☐ Form 8839 c ☐ Form 8859	
55	Other credits: a ☐ Form 3800 b ☐ Form 8801 c ☐ Form	
56	Add lines 47 through 55. These are your total credits	2,000
57	Subtract line 56 from line 46. If line 56 is more than line 46, enter -0- ▶	1,054

Standard Deduction for—
- People who checked any box on line 39a or 39b or who can be claimed as a dependent, see page 34.
- All others:
Single or Married filing separately, $5,150
Married filing jointly or Qualifying widow(er), $10,300
Head of household, $7,550

Other Taxes

Line	Description	Amount
58	Self-employment tax. Attach Schedule SE	
59	Social security and Medicare tax on tip income not reported to employer. Attach Form 4137	
60	Additional tax on IRAs, other qualified retirement plans, etc. Attach Form 5329 if required	
61	Advance earned income credit payments from Form(s) W-2, box 9	
62	Household employment taxes. Attach Schedule H	
63	Add lines 57 through 62. This is your total tax ▶	1,054

Payments

If you have a qualifying child, attach Schedule EIC.

Line	Description	Amount
64	Federal income tax withheld from Forms W-2 and 1099	
65	2006 estimated tax payments and amount applied from 2005 return	
66a	Earned income credit (EIC)	
b	Nontaxable combat pay election ▶ 66b	
67	Excess social security and tier 1 RRTA tax withheld (see page 60)	
68	Additional child tax credit. Attach Form 8812	
69	Amount paid with request for extension to file (see page 60)	
70	Payments from: a ☐ Form 2439 b ☐ Form 4136 c ☐ Form 8885	
71	Credit for federal telephone excise tax paid. Attach Form 8913 if required	
72	Add lines 64, 65, 66a, and 67 through 71. These are your total payments ▶	

Refund

Direct deposit? See page 61 and fill in 74b, 74c, and 74d, or Form 8888.

Line	Description	Amount
73	If line 72 is more than line 63, subtract line 63 from line 72. This is the amount you overpaid	
74a	Amount of line 73 you want refunded to you. If Form 8888 is attached, check here ▶ ☐	
b	Routing number: X X X X X X X X X c Type: ☐ Checking ☐ Savings	
d	Account number: X X X X X X X X X X X X X X X X X	
75	Amount of line 73 you want applied to your 2007 estimated tax ▶	

Amount You Owe

Line	Description	Amount
76	Amount you owe. Subtract line 72 from line 63. For details on how to pay, see page 62 ▶	1,054
77	Estimated tax penalty (see page 62)	

Third Party Designee

Do you want to allow another person to discuss this return with the IRS (see page 63)? ☐ Yes. Complete the following. ✓ No

Designee's name ▶   Phone no. ▶ ( )   Personal identification number (PIN) ▶

Sign Here

Joint return? See page 17. Keep a copy for your records.

Under penalties of perjury, I declare that I have examined this return and accompanying schedules and statements, and to the best of my knowledge and belief, they are true, correct, and complete. Declaration of preparer (other than taxpayer) is based on all information of which preparer has any knowledge.

Your signature | Date | Your occupation | Daytime phone number ( )
Spouse's signature. If a joint return, both must sign. | Date | Spouse's occupation |

Paid Preparer's Use Only

Preparer's signature ▶ | Date | Check if self-employed ☐ | Preparer's SSN or PTIN
Firm's name (or yours if self-employed), address, and ZIP code ▶ | | EIN | Phone no. ( )

Form **1040** (2006)

Taxpayer #4 page 1

Form 1040 — U.S. Individual Income Tax Return 2006

Department of the Treasury—Internal Revenue Service
For the year Jan. 1–Dec. 31, 2006, or other tax year beginning , 2006, ending , 20
OMB No. 1545-0074

Label

Your first name and initial: **WINDEL** Last name: **H**
Your social security number: **111 11 111**

If a joint return, spouse's first name and initial: **WINDY** Last name: **H**
Spouse's social security number: **444 44 4444**

Home address:

City, town or post office, state, and ZIP code: **APOPKA, FL 32712**

Filing Status: 2 ✓ Married filing jointly (even if only one had income)

Exemptions
- 6a ✓ Yourself
- 6b ✓ Spouse
- 6c Dependents:
(1) First/Last name	(2) SSN	(3) Relationship	(4) Qualifying child for child tax credit
SHERRY H	222 22 2222	daughter	✓
DONALD H	333 33 3333	son	✓

Boxes checked on 6a and 6b: **2**
No. of children on 6c who lived with you: **2**
Add numbers on lines above: **4**

Income

Line	Description	Amount
7	Wages, salaries, tips, etc. Attach Form(s) W-2	480,000
22	Total income	480,000
37	Adjusted gross income	480,000

Form 1040 (2006) Cat. No. 11320B

66

Taxpayer #4 page 2

Form 1040 (2006) Page 2

Tax and Credits

Line	Description	Amount
38	Amount from line 37 (adjusted gross income)	480,000
39a	Check if: You were born before January 2, 1942, ☐ Blind. Spouse was born before January 2, 1942, ☐ Blind. Total boxes checked ▶ 39a	
39b	If your spouse itemizes on a separate return or you were a dual-status alien, see page 34 and check here ▶39b ☐	
40	Itemized deductions (from Schedule A) or your standard deduction (see left margin)	10,000
41	Subtract line 40 from line 38	470,000
42	If line 38 is over $112,875, or you provided housing to a person displaced by Hurricane Katrina, see page 36. Otherwise, multiply $3,300 by the total number of exemptions claimed on line 6d	
43	**Taxable income.** Subtract line 42 from line 41. If line 42 is more than line 41, enter -0-	470,000
44	Tax (see page 36). Check if any tax is from: a ☐ Form(s) 8814 b ☐ Form 4972	138,563
45	Alternative minimum tax (see page 39). Attach Form 6251	
46	Add lines 44 and 45	138,563
47	Foreign tax credit. Attach Form 1116 if required	
48	Credit for child and dependent care expenses. Attach Form 2441	
49	Credit for the elderly or the disabled. Attach Schedule R	
50	Education credits. Attach Form 8863	
51	Retirement savings contributions credit. Attach Form 8880	
52	Residential energy credits. Attach Form 5695	
53	Child tax credit (see page 42). Attach Form 8901 if required	
54	Credits from: a ☐ Form 8396 b ☐ Form 8839 c ☐ Form 8859	
55	Other credits: a ☐ Form 3800 b ☐ Form 8801 c ☐ Form ___	
56	Add lines 47 through 55. These are your **total credits**	
57	Subtract line 56 from line 46. If line 56 is more than line 46, enter -0-	138,563

Standard Deduction for—
- People who checked any box on line 39a or 39b **or** who can be claimed as a dependent, see page 34.
- All others:
  Single or Married filing separately, $5,150
  Married filing jointly or Qualifying widow(er), $10,300
  Head of household, $7,550

Other Taxes

Line	Description	Amount
58	Self-employment tax. Attach Schedule SE	
59	Social security and Medicare tax on tip income not reported to employer. Attach Form 4137	
60	Additional tax on IRAs, other qualified retirement plans, etc. Attach Form 5329 if required	
61	Advance earned income credit payments from Form(s) W-2, box 9	
62	Household employment taxes. Attach Schedule H	
63	Add lines 57 through 62. This is your **total tax**	138,563

Payments

Line	Description	Amount
64	Federal income tax withheld from Forms W-2 and 1099	
65	2006 estimated tax payments and amount applied from 2005 return	
66a	Earned income credit (EIC)	
66b	Nontaxable combat pay election ▶	
67	Excess social security and tier 1 RRTA tax withheld (see page 60)	
68	Additional child tax credit. Attach Form 8812	
69	Amount paid with request for extension to file (see page 60)	
70	Payments from: a ☐ Form 2439 b ☐ Form 4136 c ☐ Form 8885	
71	Credit for federal telephone excise tax paid. Attach Form 8913 if required	
72	Add lines 64, 65, 66a, and 67 through 71. These are your **total payments**	

If you have a qualifying child, attach Schedule EIC.

Refund

73. If line 72 is more than line 63, subtract line 63 from line 72. This is the amount you **overpaid**
74a. Amount of line 73 you want **refunded to you.** If Form 8888 is attached, check here ▶ ☐
b. Routing number: X X X X X X X X X ▶ c Type: ☐ Checking ☐ Savings
d. Account number: X X X X X X X X X X X X X X X X X
75. Amount of line 73 you want **applied to your 2007 estimated tax** ▶ 75

Direct deposit? See page 61 and fill in 74b, 74c, and 74d, or Form 8888.

Amount You Owe

76. **Amount you owe.** Subtract line 72 from line 63. For details on how to pay, see page 62 ▶ | 138,563
77. Estimated tax penalty (see page 62)

Third Party Designee

Do you want to allow another person to discuss this return with the IRS (see page 63)? ☐ **Yes.** Complete the following. ✓ **No**
Designee's name ▶   Phone no. ▶ (   )   Personal identification number (PIN) ▶

Sign Here

Under penalties of perjury, I declare that I have examined this return and accompanying schedules and statements, and to the best of my knowledge and belief, they are true, correct, and complete. Declaration of preparer (other than taxpayer) is based on all information of which preparer has any knowledge.

Your signature | Date | Your occupation | Daytime phone number
Spouse's signature. If a joint return, **both** must sign. | Date | Spouse's occupation |

Joint return? See page 17. Keep a copy for your records.

Paid Preparer's Use Only

Preparer's signature ▶   Date   Check if self-employed ☐   Preparer's SSN or PTIN
Firm's name (or yours if self-employed), address, and ZIP code ▶   EIN   Phone no. (   )

Form **1040** (2006)

Taxpayer #5 page 1

Form 1040 — U.S. Individual Income Tax Return 2006

Department of the Treasury—Internal Revenue Service
For the year Jan. 1–Dec. 31, 2006, or other tax year beginning , 2006, ending , 20
OMB No. 1545-0074

Label

Your first name and initial: WINDEL H
If a joint return, spouse's first name and initial: WINDY H
Home address: (blank)
City, town or post office, state, and ZIP code: APOPKA, FL 32712

Your social security number: 111-11-111
Spouse's social security number: 444-44-4444

Presidential Election Campaign: (not checked)

Filing Status: 2 ✓ Married filing jointly

Exemptions:
- 6a ✓ Yourself
- 6b ✓ Spouse
- 6c Dependents:
  - SHERRY H, 222-22-2222, daughter, ✓ child tax credit
  - DONALD H, 333-33-3333, son, ✓ child tax credit
- Boxes checked on 6a and 6b: 2
- No. of children on 6c who lived with you: 2
- Add numbers on lines above: 4

Income
- 7 Wages, salaries, tips, etc.: 4,800,000
- 22 Total income: 4,800,000

Adjusted Gross Income
- 37 Adjusted gross income: 4,800,000

Cat. No. 11320B   Form **1040** (2006)

Taxpayer #5 page 2

Form 1040 (2006) — Page 2

Tax and Credits

Line	Description	Amount
38	Amount from line 37 (adjusted gross income)	4,800,000
39a	Check if: You were born before January 2, 1942, ☐ Blind. Spouse was born before January 2, 1942, ☐ Blind. Total boxes checked ▶ 39a	
39b	If your spouse itemizes on a separate return or you were a dual-status alien, see page 34 and check here ▶ 39b ☐	
40	Itemized deductions (from Schedule A) or your standard deduction (see left margin)	10,000
41	Subtract line 40 from line 38	4,790,000
42	If line 38 is over $112,875, or you provided housing to a person displaced by Hurricane Katrina, see page 36. Otherwise, multiply $3,300 by the total number of exemptions claimed on line 6d	
43	Taxable income. Subtract line 42 from line 41. If line 42 is more than line 41, enter -0-	4,790,000
44	Tax (see page 36). Check if any tax is from: a ☐ Form(s) 8814 b ☐ Form 4972	1,650,563
45	Alternative minimum tax (see page 39). Attach Form 6251	
46	Add lines 44 and 45	1,650,563
47	Foreign tax credit. Attach Form 1116 if required	
48	Credit for child and dependent care expenses. Attach Form 2441	
49	Credit for the elderly or the disabled. Attach Schedule R	
50	Education credits. Attach Form 8863	
51	Retirement savings contributions credit. Attach Form 8880	
52	Residential energy credits. Attach Form 5695	
53	Child tax credit (see page 42). Attach Form 8901 if required	
54	Credits from: a ☐ Form 8396 b ☐ Form 8839 c ☐ Form 8859	
55	Other credits: a ☐ Form 3800 b ☐ Form 8801 c ☐ Form ___	
56	Add lines 47 through 55. These are your total credits	
57	Subtract line 56 from line 46. If line 56 is more than line 46, enter -0-	1,650,563

Other Taxes

Line	Description	Amount
58	Self-employment tax. Attach Schedule SE	
59	Social security and Medicare tax on tip income not reported to employer. Attach Form 4137	
60	Additional tax on IRAs, other qualified retirement plans, etc. Attach Form 5329 if required	
61	Advance earned income credit payments from Form(s) W-2, box 9	
62	Household employment taxes. Attach Schedule H	
63	Add lines 57 through 62. This is your total tax	1,650,563

Payments

Line	Description	Amount
64	Federal income tax withheld from Forms W-2 and 1099	
65	2006 estimated tax payments and amount applied from 2005 return	
66a	Earned income credit (EIC)	
66b	Nontaxable combat pay election ▶	
67	Excess social security and tier 1 RRTA tax withheld (see page 60)	
68	Additional child tax credit. Attach Form 8812	
69	Amount paid with request for extension to file (see page 60)	
70	Payments from: a ☐ Form 2439 b ☐ Form 4136 c ☐ Form 8885	
71	Credit for federal telephone excise tax paid. Attach Form 8913 if required	
72	Add lines 64, 65, 66a, and 67 through 71. These are your total payments	

Refund

Line	Description	Amount
73	If line 72 is more than line 63, subtract line 63 from line 72. This is the amount you overpaid	
74a	Amount of line 73 you want refunded to you. If Form 8888 is attached, check here ▶ ☐	
74b	Routing number: X X X X X X X X X c Type: ☐ Checking ☐ Savings	
74d	Account number: X X X X X X X X X X X X X X X X X	
75	Amount of line 73 you want applied to your 2007 estimated tax ▶	

Amount You Owe

Line	Description	Amount
76	Amount you owe. Subtract line 72 from line 63. For details on how to pay, see page 62 ▶	1,650,563
77	Estimated tax penalty (see page 62)	

Third Party Designee: Do you want to allow another person to discuss this return with the IRS (see page 63)? ☐ Yes. Complete the following. ✓ No

Standard Deduction for—
- People who checked any box on line 39a or 39b or who can be claimed as a dependent, see page 34.
- All others:
  Single or Married filing separately, $5,150
  Married filing jointly or Qualifying widow(er), $10,300
  Head of household, $7,550

Form 1040 (2006)

Made in the USA
Lexington, KY
05 December 2017